CONTENTS

LIBRARY PROGRAMMING FOR FAMILIES WITH YOUNG CHILDREN

A How-To-Do-It Manual

SUE McCLEAF NESPECA

HOW-TO-DO-IT MANUALS
FOR LIBRARIANS

Number 45

NEAL-SCHUMAN PUBLISHERS, INC.
New York, London

Published by Neal-Schuman Publishers, Inc.
100 Varick Street
New York, NY 10013

Printed and bound in the United States of America

Library of Congress Cataloging-in-Publication Data

Nespeca , Sue McCleaf .
    Library programming for families with young children / by Sue McCleaf Nespeca .
        p.   cm. -- (A how-to-do-it manual ; no . 45)
    Includes bibliographical references and index .
    ISBN 1-55570-181-7
      1. Libraries and families--United States .   2 .Children ' s
libraries--Activity programs--United States.   3. Public libraries-
-Cultural programs--United States . I. Title.   II. Series :   How - to
 - do - it manuals for libraries ; no. 45.
    Z711 . 9 . . F34N47   1994
    027 . 62 ' 5--dc20   94-37894
                                                                    CIP

ACKNOWLEDGMENTS

I would like to express my gratitude to my editor, Virginia Mathews, for her advice and encouragement. Special thanks to: Kelly Kroll, who assisted with proofing and editing; Joan Reeve, for her knowledge and suggestions for Chapter Two; and my husband Gil, for his support and patience.

Thanks also to the following publishers for allowing me to include their fingerplays in my sample programs: the fingerplays "Busy Fingers" and "Ten Little Fingers" reprinted from "Ring a Ring o' Roses," published by the Flint Public Library, 1026 E. Kearsley Street, Flint, MI 48502 (810) 232-7111; and the fingerplay "Up the Hill" from *Trot Trot to Boston!* by Carol Ra copyright 1987 by Carol Ra by permission of Lothrop, Lee and Shepard Books, a division of William Morrow and Co. Inc.

INTRODUCTION

As we quickly approach a new century, libraries continue to face changing demographic, societal, and economic conditions that demand a reassessment of goals and reason for existence. Technology alone is causing libraries to rethink services and ways to expend limited funds. And yet many service patterns and programs remain consistent with those from the middle of this century. Emphasis in the past has been on ways in which we can serve our customers better, rather than how we can serve those who are not already using our resources.

During these tight economic times for libraries, it is even more important that we justify our existence to legislators and tax-payers. A mission statement or a role as only a popular materials center, or a center for recreational reading, is not perceived as being worthy of community support. Libraries must be seen as a necessary component for formal and informal learning for a lifetime.

There are various roles that fit the educational component, but probably none is as vital as the "Preschooler's Door to Learning," as ascribed in *Planning and Role Setting for Public Libraries* by the American Library Association. For future adult members of the society to become regular library users and to see the library as an institution that they do not want to do without, a pattern of library use must be established at a young age, during the preschool years if possible. Young children cannot develop this pattern on their own; it must be modeled by parents/families or other caregivers. Family units today can be defined in many ways, but all the caregiver/s of the young child will have a lasting influence on that child's literacy development. Early childhood is a critical period for developing language skills that are the basis for literacy, and there is no greater indicator for success than the degree of parental or family involvement.

Libraries need to build on individual family strengths by including the entire family in programming for young children. Libraries must also reexamine traditional methods of service. Probably the most typical program in public libraries today is preschool storytime. This staple began as part of library programming in the 1930's, and became commonplace in the fifties. Many libraries still hold two, four, six or more preschool storytimes a week year-round to the same group of children, most often with the children alone, and the caregiver in a different room, similar to what was done in the fifties. Some libraries balance these preschool storytimes with at least one session of family storytime.

No one seems to question why we have programmed the same way for over forty years. Children entered a separate room without a caregiver for storytime in the 50's, 60's and 70's because for many children, this was their first independent experience without Mom at hand. That is rarely the case in the 90's, however. Many children encounter independent experiences away from their Mom or caregiver from infancy. It is more important now that storytimes are enjoyed by the young child with family close at hand. Librarians trained in serving young children are excellent models for many types of literacy experiences. With family members participating, the librarian can be an encouraging example of how to read, share stories, talk and sing with young children. Librarians can enhance language skills and listening experiences, and inspire caregivers with ways to share art and dramatic play. Instead of segregating parents or caregivers, we should invite them to participate in our story programs. What about offering two, four, six or more storytimes a week year-round?

Why do we put so much staff time in a program for one age group, rather than an equal number of preschool programs balanced by the same number of programs for infants, toddlers, early primary-aged children etc.? And instead of serving the same children over and over again year-round, why not reach new children, those children who may need us the most, the children not already walking through our door? We need to evaluate why we are doing certain programs, the number of programs we are doing, the ways we market ourselves, and our methods of service. Traditional programming needs to be reexamined, not necessarily to change it completely, but to reevaluate what our purpose is for doing a certain program, and what are our goals. To continue the way we always have, even if a program is presently successful, does not really allow for growth, nor does it guarantee future success, and it really might not be meeting the needs of all the people we should be trying to serve.

Goal One of the National Educational Goals states that all children in America will start school ready to learn by the year 2000. Though we know that all children are ready to learn from birth, librarians can play a vital role in assisting families with very young children's emerging literacy skills. Parenting programs for mothers/caregivers of infants can train these Moms, often teens, to develop their babies' learning abilities.

My interest has always been in the education of the young child, so much so, that I decided to obtain a second master's degree in early childhood education. While at Kent State University, I conducted a research study of parental involvement of urban Head Start mothers in their young child's emergent literacy skills. Though I had felt for a long time that family involvement was so crucial to a young child's education, the mothers I interviewed made me realize more than ever that libraries needed to make sure the family became a more integral part of library programming. In addition, I began to realize the importance of outreach to families. This precipitated me into writing, in 1990, my first article for *School Library Journal* on "Reaching the Unserved: Libraries Can Attack Illiteracy." After attending a library conference and speaking to probably the foremost authority in the nation on why young children need libraries, my editor, Virginia Mathews, encouraged me to write this book.

It is my hope that librarians serving youth in our nation will consider the entire family when planning programs for young children. That is why there are so many different types of programs described in this book. Few librarians will be able to do *all* of the programs or types of outreach, but I hope this book will inspire you to add caregivers in even one or two programs for young children in which you have not included them previously.

For libraries aspiring to the role of "Preschooler's Door to Learning," this book can be used as a guidebook for that purpose. Librarians are generally very successful at matching up young children with books. It is important however to understand why certain books are more appropriate at certain stages, and it is for this reason, a chapter is devoted to the developmental characteristics of young children. Members of the early care and education community that subscribe to the views of their national organization, the National Association for the Education of Young Children, know the importance of developmentally appropriate curriculum. Librarians also need to know what is developmentally appropriate when planning library programs.

There are ideas for programming to caregivers on the importance of reading aloud, and for those caregivers who cannot read, the necessity of family literacy programs. Samples of infant, toddler and preschool storytimes with caregivers present and participating are given as examples. Some libraries are very short staffed and can only do programs for families with young children of mixed age groups. Other libraries are able to do storytimes that are more developmentally appropriate for individual age groups, but also like to have additional evening family storytime programs. Examples of various mixed age group family programs are given. Family history, multicultural and intergenerational programs, which build on the strength of the family unit, are also included. The last two chapters address the importance of outreach to the early care and education community and to the diverse special populations in the library's service area.

Many libraries are already including families in their library programs but will hopefully find other ideas to try. And for others, I hope you will be inspired to try some new family programs. I would love to hear about your successful efforts. Happy family programming!

1 THE IMPORTANCE OF FAMILY LIBRARY PROGRAMMING

WHAT IS FAMILY LIBRARY PROGRAMMING?

Family library programming for young children recognizes the role of the entire family unit, particularly the involvement of the caregiver(s), in improving the emerging literacy skills of the young child. Without family involvement from birth, young children are not exposed early enough to literature and have fewer ways to increase their language and listening skills. Because educators realize that this early involvement affects a child's later efforts at learning to read, helps establish that child's subsequent joy in reading, and has an effect on the child's future success in school, few can argue the importance of this involvement.

One early book that stressed the importance of involving parents in programs for young children was *Start Early for an Early Start: You and the Young Child.*[1] This book, now considered a classic in the library world, proved an impetus for involving parents in storytime programs. Beginning in the late 1970s and to the present, many public libraries held toddler and more recently infant storytimes for the express purpose of involving caregivers in the young child's emerging literacy abilities. Some public libraries, and several school libraries, have extended this during the 1990s to recognize the significance of the familial unit in planning all types of family activities, from family story programs to family history programs, intergenerational programs, and outreach programs. A wave of family library programming has begun, and it is the purpose of this book to encourage public and school librarians to consider this type of programming a top priority during the 1990s and beyond.

Traditional programming methods, such as preschool storytimes without caregivers that have been used since the 1960s, need to be changed for the sole reason of improving the literacy of the entire family and to help achieve national educational goals. For those libraries that have chosen the "Preschooler's Door to Learning" (from *Planning and Role Setting for Public Libraries* by the American Library Association) as one of their roles in their mission statement, family library programming is a given. The role is defined as: "The library encourages young children to develop an interest in reading and learning through services for children, and for parents and children together."[2]

A DEFINITION OF "FAMILY"

What is a family? A family, as defined in this book, is any unit of people, with at least one adult and one child, who recognize themselves as a familial unit, though not necessarily related by law or by blood. It can include a young child's siblings, aunts, uncles, grandparents, guardians or a foster parent. It can be people sharing living quarters, or a young child who only sees a parent on occasion. Families can be single-parent households, extended families, "blended" families, or homes with two adults of the same sex raising a child. Whatever the case, family library programming recognizes the family unit as the young child's primary socialization agent and that the effect of any library program is valuable only if the experience is reinforced at home. For the purposes of this book, the adult in the family will be labeled the "caregiver" of the young child.

WHY DO LIBRARY PROGRAMMING FOR THE ENTIRE FAMILY?

Family structures have obviously changed dramatically over the years. The conventional two-parent family with the father as the sole breadwinner is now the minority. Two-parent families now are usually dual-income, or in numerous cases, the mother is the breadwinner. Thus there is often a lack of time and energy to devote to parental involvement in young children's early home education. Single-parent households abound, and many families struggle with economic and other societal problems. Almost one in four American children younger than six lived in poverty in

1990.[3] These poor children are less likely than others to attend quality child care or preschool programs. Families also are much more mobile, and it is not as common as it once was to live close to extended family members who can help with child care.

Crime, violence, and disregard for others' race, rights, feelings, and possessions have increased in all walks of life. More families are fearful and less trusting not only of those who reside near them, but also of authority figures. There also seems to be less of a feeling of responsibility or caring for other people's children, as there is in some other societies. With so many pressures facing families today, problems associated with illiteracy may seem like one small ripple in a sea of problems.

What is the role of the public library or school library in a family's literacy efforts? Do we have a responsibility to reach out to those who could use some assistance in the education of their young children? Or do we sit idly by and continue to serve those who already know the importance of reading to their young children, and would come to the library with or without the encouragement of our programming efforts? Even preschool storytimes with caregivers present may have little effect if reinforcement and guidance does not continue at home. And there is no better way to stimulate this type of reinforcement or guidance than by modeling techniques to caregivers who are present while we are programming. We can augment what they already know about the importance of sharing books, language, rhymes, poetry, music, creative dramatics, art, story writing, and creating books. We can provide advice and encouragement to families who feel they have little time or energy. It is a big goal, but by no means an insurmountable one. A change in focus and an emphasis on outreach can only lead to more productive library programming.

The United Nations General Assembly proclaimed 1994 as the "International Year of the Family." The theme of the year was "Family: Resources and Responsibilities in a Changing World." The emphasis was to strengthen the family's ability to meet its own needs. One of the goals was to make families aware of what they can expect in the way of services provided by public institutions. Libraries need to carry on this initiative by making families cognizant of their services, whether it be family library programs or family literacy programs, which enable adults who need help in learning to read. There is much government emphasis on the family and ways the family can be involved in improving its quality of life.

Public schools are actively pursuing more ways to enlist parental involvement in the education of young children. Research has proposed that discontinuity between home and school is the major cause of low academic achievement of ethnic minority children, low-income children, and children of parents with relatively few years of education.[4] Thus, more direct and meaningful involvement by parents in their children's education in ways other than parent-teacher conferences, open houses, or fund-raising efforts is needed at schools. Students' achievement improves when caregivers are partners in their children's education. When caregivers become actively involved, their children realize that they value education. Libraries in turn can profit from the knowledge gleaned by educators on the benefits of family involvement.

Early childhood intervention programs in place even from the turn of the century have been based on three assumptions about child development:

> "1. early childhood is a critically important time in an individual's development; 2. the home is the crucial place for early development to take place, with the corollary that the mother (primary caregiver) is the child's most significant teacher; and 3. the parents of young children need and will use advice and support with child rearing."[5]

These programs reinforce the belief that the caregiver is the child's first teacher. In the case of family library programming, the caregiver may not only be the teacher, but also the learner. A leader in theories of early childhood development, Urie Bronfenbrenner, vocal on the subject of the influence of the family on the young child, stated that "the involvement of the child's family as an active participant is critical to the success to any intervention program."[6]

The National Educational Goals outlined and endorsed by our nation's governors and President in 1989,[7] and former President Bush's America 2000 strategy[8] are other considerations as libraries ascertain their role in the community. The first National Educational Goal states: "All children in America will start school ready to learn by the year 2000." Barbara K. Stripling in *Libraries for the National Education Goals*[9] has clearly defined ways libraries can assist the nation in reaching this first goal through family library programming.

> "Library programs for preschool children are more effective if they involve parents, family members, and caregivers; these programs also provide opportunities for parent education." (p. 10)

"Library programs for preschool children use promotion and outreach to involve traditional library nonusers." (p. 10)

"Once they have participated in library activity, the parents and preschoolers are likely to continue to check out books and attend activities throughout the year." (p. 10)

"Infant/toddler lapsit programs involve parents in all the activities with their children. Comprehension of children participating in these programs improves steadily; early language acquisition is facilitated." (p. 11)

"Parents of children who have participated in preschool programs continue to foster the love and value of reading in their children, even after the children have entered school." (p. 12)

"By targeting disadvantaged families with preschool reading programs, librarians can establish a pattern of having books and reading aloud in the home. If free books are offered, they inspire parents who typically do not use the library to read to their preschoolers; other children in the family also enjoy the new books." (p. 15)

"Librarians can break the cycle of illiteracy by teaching parents how to help their children develop." (p. 15)

"Parents who participate in weekly preschool programs with their children usually receive handouts of the activities, have a chance to practice them with a librarian to guide them, and then can repeat them with their children at home." (p. 16)

"Preschool programs that involve parents can become a social event with the parents. Networks among parents with small children are formed; the networks provide support, shared information, and impetus to continue with reading activities." (p. 16)

"Public libraries encourage new parents' enthusiasm for reading through programs that offer training, tips, books, and incentives for reading to their newborn children." (p. 16)

"Workshops for child care providers help these caregivers to begin reading aloud programs during the day. Libraries provide bibliographies, activity sheets, and sometimes even collections of books for parents to borrow from as they pick up their children." (p. 16)

"Libraries may target teen parents with programs to encourage them to read to their new babies. Workshops can be held to teach the parents how to read aloud, what books are the most fun to share, and which activities and songs are appropriate for different age levels." (p. 17)

"Library programs may target at-risk parents, offering them exposure to picture books and visually appealing concept books, practice at finger plays and nursery rhymes, discussion about the value of reading, and a selection of audio visual materials. These programs are often held at locations other than the library . . . for the convenience of the parents. Such programs cause parents to begin sharing books with their at-risk preschoolers at home." (p. 22)

"Intergenerational literacy programs have been successful at achieving their goals: helping parents understand the importance of modeling, improving the parents' reading skills, enhancing the reading readiness of preschoolers, and improving the self-esteem of the parents and children." (p. 24)

In addition to libraries fulfilling their mission statement through the "Preschooler's Door to Learning" role, or ascribing to the National Education Goals and supporting the public schools in their efforts to increase the involvement of parents in their child's education, libraries can collaborate with the federal Head Start program and its achievement in empowering caregivers. In *Head Start: The Inside Story of America's Most Successful Educational Experiment*, success stories abound of parents who started out without even a high-school diploma, became involved as parent volunteers in Head Start, later becoming leaders on Policy Committees and ending up with a college degree.[10] The involvement of parents in the Head Start program clearly has a positive effect in encouraging them to obtain training in child development.[11] In addition, objectives that guide the educational program of Head Start emphatically state the importance of parental involvement:

"1. Involve parents in educational activities of the program to enhance their role as the principal influence on the child's education and development; 2. Assist parents to increase their knowledge, understanding, skills, and experience in growth and development; 3. Identify and reinforce experiences that occur in the home that parents can utilize as educational activities for their children."[12]

Because of the accomplishments of the Head Start program in the empowering of parents, it was particularly fortuitous that the

Library-Head Start Partnership Project was established in 1992. The project of the Center for the Book in the Library of Congress, the Head Start Bureau of the U.S. Department of Health and Human Services, and the Association for Library Service to Children of the American Library Association was designed to "demonstrate in communities nationwide how libraries that serve young children can plan and work with Head Start grantees/classrooms to enhance learning and parent involvement in children's literacy and language development."[13] Because libraries nationwide will be involved in this project for years to come, family library programming is a natural outgrowth of this project.

HOW TO DO PROGRAMMING FOR THE ENTIRE FAMILY

This book will serve as a guide for the various types of programs that can be offered for the family, whether it be the caregiver and one child, or two caregivers and several children in the same family. The emphasis is on young children, from infancy through third grade. However, several of the programs will have interest to children older than third grade. This book is just a starting point, however, as there are many other examples of family library programs that can be offered. The programs presented here can serve as models for more typical programs.

OVERCOMING OBSTACLES TO FAMILY LIBRARY PROGRAMMING

Often libraries are hesitant to commit to a new form of programming due to an overextended schedule already in place in the youth-services department. In times of declining budgets, shrinking staff, and limited library hours, the very thought of beginning a new service or program is quickly dismissed. Yet, these same libraries rarely stop preschool storytimes. In some areas, libraries have from two to as many as eight preschool programs a week. Those who attend the preschool storytimes are often from families that already know the importance of reading to their young child, and would come to the library for books without scheduled storytimes, albeit perhaps less frequently. Those caregivers who most need to understand the importance of participating in their children's education and of reading to young children from birth; who need help in choosing books; and who most need to learn *how* to read to young children probably never set foot in the library. So the libraries' extensive preschool programming is reaching those who need it the least, and low-literacy caregivers are often virtually ignored.

It is difficult to make changes in programming that is popular and has been successful for some time. Yet public libraries need to take into account the changes occurring in society and consider how they can best serve *all* the people in their community, rather than just a select few. Such decisions may not be popular with library directors or board members, and may have some effect on circulation statistics. But libraries must assess their role in terms of their community and determine who they best need to serve.

Several libraries have overcome the obstacle of trying to reach more people with less staff and fewer dollars by training volunteers (often senior citizens or members of a Friends of the Library group) in storytelling. After several training sessions, these individuals visit children in day-care centers, preschools, and other settings, reaching children who may have little exposure to the public library. Other libraries have distributed kits of books and materials such as puppets, learning games, and the like to early childhood centers and then train educators or caregivers in the use of the kits. This is one way of reaching more children. These ideas will be elaborated on in Chapter 7 of this book.

Libraries need to consider other access issues in their community. Many caregivers lack transportation to the library or money for public transportation. In some cities, public transportation runs only during daylight hours, and if libraries are only open one or two nights a week, users can be frustrated even trying to get to the library. One solution is the bookmobile, one that goes not just to rural areas, but also in large cities to poor neighborhoods where people have few easy modes of transportation. Another library staple, the mail-a-book program, is usually restricted to rural areas. These services should be expanded to those unable to get to the library easily due to transportation or time constraints.

Many caregivers work during the daytime, the most common time for public library programs to be held. Many libraries have adjusted this schedule and hold family library programs during the evening or on weekends. But with budget cuts, libraries' evening and weekend hours are often cut, a direct denial of access for many potential users. Libraries need to reconsider the needs of their customers when scheduling hours and programs. Libraries unable to change hours will need to make extra efforts to reach early childhood educators and teachers who have access to most of the children in the community. This will be discussed more fully in Chapter 7.

For a research project I conducted with Head Start parents for Kent State University in 1991, I found that many low-income families are afraid to check out library books for fear their children will damage them and they would be unable to pay. Others feared fines for overdue materials. Some libraries have overcome this problem by not charging fines to children. The Enoch Pratt Library in Baltimore is considering allowing children to help shelve books or to prepare for children's programs instead of paying fines. These solutions answer the problem of fines, but the fear of damaging materials and being unable to pay for them is not really resolved. Book giveaway programs address this problem to a degree, but this still does not expose the children to a wide variety of books at progressive reading levels.

A major problem involved with outreach is the attempt to reach families in which the caregivers themselves cannot read. Libraries should consider family literacy programs to meet the needs of these families. This requires cooperation between two departments in the library, adult and children's services. Often caregivers are being taught to read while young children are read stories. Others enroll parents, families, and children in shared reading and storytelling activities. More will be mentioned on family literacy programs in Chapter 3.

One also needs to consider the "724 children" described by George Will in a Newsweek article. These are children kept at home, indoors, seven days a week, 24 hours a day, because their neighborhoods are filled with drugs, violence, and murder.[14] Boston City Hospital's Pediatric Primary Care Center "treats" some of these children of poverty by giving them books—believing that reading together can be therapy for families living under stress. Training and resources are provided to pediatricians, residents, and nurse practitioners. In a project called "Reach Out and Read," Dr. Robert Needlman and Kathleen Fitzgerald Rice have volunteers read to children in waiting rooms and have pediatricians in primary-care clinics give away picture books at check-up visits and prescribe to parents that reading to children is important for their health. They firmly believe that parents who had been given a book by a pediatrician were "four times as likely as parents who had not, to say they had looked at books with their children over the past 24 hours, or to list looking at books as among their children's three favorite activities."[15] Author Rosemary Wells states decisively in an article in *Horn Book* that "Children's books must be advertised directly to the public as part of a healthy lifestyle." She mentions a campaign that has the support of the Association of Booksellers for Children, the American Booksellers Association, and others, which endorses reading aloud to children with the slogan "The Most Important Twenty Minutes of Your Day." One point included in the campaign is: "We need to urge American pediatricians to promote reading to children as a regular daily routine, just as dental hygiene, basic nutrition, and inoculation against childhood diseases are promoted."[16]

In the research project done with Head Start Parents for Kent State University, mentioned previously, the most amazing interview was with an urban Head Start parent, here to be called Jolette, who lived in the most dangerous housing project in the city. This housing project was described in the local newspaper in 1991 as follows: "Project residents tell stories of fear and violence almost too hard to believe. Children sleep on the floor to avoid stray bullets. Elderly residents shut their window shades and stay indoors, getting neighbors to run to the grocery store and post office. Drug dealers jump from rooftop to rooftop, brandishing high-powered weapons." Jolette described in an audiotaped conversation, days when her children were playing out in the front yard and she had to retrieve them, due to bullets whizzing by her house. This same mother was taped explaining her reading habits to her children. "I have books galore! I collect books, I don't throw books away. I have books in my closet, I have books on my tables, I have books stored away in my end tables, I have books in my room, I have books in their room. Books, books, books . . . " She also described her daily activities with her young Head Start children: making up dramatic plays; making up songs; doing finger plays; helping with shapes; drawing letters on a piece of paper and having the children practice; watching "Sesame Street" and "Mister Rogers' Neighborhood"; coloring with the children, etc.[17] One should never assume that poverty-stricken families do not have the desire or knowledge to read to their young children.

To be effective, family library programming must take into account the strengths, styles, and needs of individual families. This "individualized approach to building on family strengths" is the basis of successful family-support programs.[18] This may be frustrating to librarians pressed for time, who feel they can plan one type of program that will be useful for all types of families. Many typical library programs offered in public libraries are directed to middle-class families who know the importance of modeling reading habits to their young children. Every family is different, however, and one must be sensitive to the strengths and values of low-literacy or minority families.

There is no one model program that will be useful in every community or for every library. One needs to know what audience likely will attend a certain program and tailor the program to fit. Values and expectations of caregivers may be different, depending on audience composition. Many programs will need to be developed to reach those who are not already participating in library programs. After targeting a certain audience, the librarian should consider the education and available resources of the participants. Resources might include books in their home or whether the family has transportation to the library. After doing this initial analysis, one should, if possible, involve the caregivers in specifying their needs in relation to what the library can provide. This form of empowerment is vital to the success of your program. When caregivers realize that their efforts are valued, and that they play an important role in their young child's life, your family library programming will influence the lives of these families long after the program ends.

ENDNOTES

1. Preschool Services and Parent Education Committee, Children's Services Division, *Start Early for an Early Start.* (Chicago: American Library Association, 1976).
2. American Library Association, *Planning and Role Setting for Public Libraries.* (Chicago: American Library Association, 1987), p. 37.
3. Children's Defense Fund, *The State of America's Children 1992.* (Washington, D.C.: Children's Defense Fund, 1992), p. 42.
4. Douglas R. Powell, *Families and Early Childhood Programs.* (Washington, D.C.: National Association of Education of Young Children, 1989), p. 39.
5. Heather Weiss, "Family Support and Education in Early Childhood Programs," in *America's Family Support Programs,* ed. Sharon L. Kagan, Douglas R. Powell, Bernice Weissbourd, and Edward F. Zigler. (New Haven: Yale University Press, 1987), p. 138.
6. Douglas R. Powell, *Families and Early Childhood Programs.* (Washington, D.C.: National Association of Education of Young Children, 1989), p. 44.
7. *National Goals for Education* (Washington, D.C.: Executive Office of the President, 1990).
8. *America 2000: An Educational Strategy. Sourcebook.* (Washington, D.C.: U.S. Department of Education, 1991).
9. Barbara K. Stripling, *Libraries for the National Education Goals.* (Syracuse: ERIC Clearinghouse on Information Resources, 1992).

10. Edward Zigler and Susan Muenchow, *Head Start: The Inside Story of America's Most Successful Educational Experiment.* (New York: Harper-Collins, 1992), p. 115.

11. Ibid., p. 117.

12. George S. Morrison, *Early Childhood Education Today.* 5th ed. (New York: Macmillan, 1991).

13. Virginia H. Mathews, *Guide to the Use of the Library Head Start Partnership Video for Programs and Workshops.* (Washington, D.C.: Center for the Book, Library of Congress, 1993), p. 1.

14. George F. Will, " 'Medicine' for '724 Children,' " *Newsweek,* March 22, 1993, p. 78.

15. Perri Klass, "Tackling Problems We Thought We Solved," *New York Times Magazine,* December 13, 1992, p. 61.

16. Rosemary Wells, "The Most Important Twenty Minutes of Your Day," *Horn Book,* May/June 1993, p. 309.

17. Sue McCleaf Nespeca, *Parental Involvement in Emergent Literacy Skills of Urban Head Start Children.* (Kent State University, unpublished, 1991).

18. Lois Pall Wandersman, "New Directions for Parent Education," in *America's Family Support Programs,* ed. Sharon L. Kagan, Douglas R. Powell, Bernice Weissbourd, and Edward F. Zigler. (New Haven: Yale University Press, 1987), p. 211.

2 DEVELOMENTAL CHARACTERISTICS OF YOUNG CHILDREN AND HOW THEY RELATE TO BOOK SHARING WITH SUGGESTED BOOKS AND ACTIVITIES

It is important that librarians understand principles of child development. When talking to caregivers about reading to their young children, librarians must know what type of books to suggest for children according to their age and developmental level. Also, it is crucial that librarians understand these stages of development when planning various programs for young children and their caregivers.

Each child is unique and does not necessarily develop at the same rate as another child of the same age. It is important to remember that children can not be categorized easily and that stages of development may overlap. Cognitive, language, and social development will differ, depending on the child and his or her interaction with the caregiver. However, most children will follow a developmental pattern similar to the one given in this chapter, though perhaps not at the exact ages given. Stages usually follow this pattern, and the model should be useful for librarians who do not have a background in child development.

There are three excellent resources for planning library programs and considering what is developmentally appropriate for the age of the child. Librarians should read the National Association for Education of Young Children's publication *Developmentally Appropriate Practice in Early Childhood Programs Serving Children From Birth Through Age 8*, edited by Sue Bredekamp. Ann Carlson's "schema," developed in her doctoral thesis and published in *Early Childhood Literature Sharing Programs in Libraries,* is also superb. The author stresses that library programs should be based on children's developmental levels rather than chronological age. Her charts listing developmental information are followed by implications for library programs and book sharing. A third good resource is Karen Miller's *Ages and Stages,* which lists developmental descriptions and activities for birth through eight years. All three books are listed in the bibliography at the end of this chapter, but the entire list was consulted and used to develop the following information.

There is much growth and change during the first eight years of life. For developmentally appropriate program-planning purposes, these years will be described in the following stages: birth to 18 months; 18 to 30 months (2 1/2 years); 2 1/2 to 3 1/2 years; 3 1/2 through five years; and six through eight years. The National Association for the Education of Young Children recommends that mixing children of a developmental age range of more than 18 months together for programs will require different strategies to be employed. Books and activities would need to be of varying lengths and ranges. Particularly for young children, it seems wise to avoid this. Thus the divisions given are recommended ones for program planning, because children of these ages are often at a similar developmental level.

Birth to 18 Months

Infants learn by experience, imitation of the caregiver, and through their senses of seeing, hearing, tasting, smelling, and feeling. Interaction with a caregiver is particularly important and basic trust develops. It is vital that the caregiver talks, sings, and reads to the baby from birth.

DEVELOPMENTAL CHARACTERISTICS

Early infant vision may be blurred, and it is not until children are six months to a year old that they see as well as adults. But even very young infants, as young as three or four months, can discriminate primary colors, though they cannot detect shades of color. Sharp visual contrasts, with clear distinctions between light and dark, are more easily seen, which may be why early theorists believed infants could see only black and white. Though babies are attracted by patterns that show high contrasts between dark and light, they are particularly attracted to faces and things that move. Thus a caregiver that gives a baby much attention and holds the child close to her face will stimulate and please the infant, because the caregiver's face has many moving parts.

Infants also hear well and respond to the sound of a human voice. They can recognize and discern one voice from another at a very young age. A mother's voice may be recognized by the first week and the voice of a father or other person who lives with the infant, within the second or third week. Infants respond to music, sounds, and singing and will soon be babbling and cooing on their own. Babies understand words before they talk and learn these words by adults talking, singing, or reading aloud to them. Thus it is important to read, talk, and sing to a baby often!

Very young infants lack hand/eye coordination, but their muscles develop rapidly and it is not long until they can hold up their heads and roll over. Infants like to be held and touched. Often they move their arms and legs when a human is near because they want to be picked up or touched. Thus games adults play with babies add to their delight, such as "Pat-a-Cake," "Peek-a-Boo," or "This Little Piggy," because the adult often touches their hands or feet when playing these games. At three months infants want to touch humans or objects they can see and reach, and by five months, they like to grasp objects, holding them, releasing them, and sucking them if possible. Small objects, such as books, can be held at this young age.

At six months, infants can sit with support and will throw objects. Within a few short months, they will creep and crawl and begin to pull themselves up. By ten or 11 months, the baby will walk with help, climb up stairs, wave goodbye, and drink from a cup.

By the time babies are nine to 12 months of age, they can understand many simple words and directions, such as "Give me your hand." They like to imitate words and sounds such as a cow mooing, and are able to say a few simple words clearly. They know and delight in songs and rhymes that have been repeated often. By using a thumb and forefinger, they can pick up objects and put them in and out of containers, such as blocks in a can.

At 12 to 18 months, the baby is curious about other children and likes to watch them, but prefers being around familiar people or objects. Basic words are learned, usually names of familiar objects, and one or more easy body parts can be named. A child begins to use two-word combinations, called telegraphic speech. (Example: "Mommy home.") In telegraphic speech, children use just content words and omit less meaningful parts of speech, such as articles and prepositions. These are young children's first sentences. The imitation of speech and action is still common. Young children will watch and listen while others are speaking and absorb more language than they can speak. Simple memory is also developing at this time. Fine motor skills are being tuned, and the child can stack blocks. Large muscles are also developing, and during this time the child learns to walk. Being curious, the child delights in exploring objects in view. Again, the child relies on senses when learning by touching, smelling, or tasting objects.

Between 16 and 18 months, the child can scribble with a crayon, often vertically or horizontally. The child can also help turn the pages of a book. Walking, climbing, carrying objects from place to place, and moving or swaying to music is quite common. The child is still attached to the caregiver and demands much personal attention, but is becoming somewhat assertive.

IMPLICATIONS FOR BOOK SHARING AND ACTIVITIES

Caregivers need to talk to, sing to, and read to their children from infancy. First books for infants should be made of heavy cardboard with rounded edges. These books are durable, washable, and can be chewed on with little damage. Colors in illustrations should be bright, because infants can not distinguish shades immediately. Pictures should show definite contrasts between light and dark, such as black and white, and definite contrasts between different colors. Familiar objects should be depicted, one object per page, or at the very least the pictures should be uncluttered. Books that show faces of various ages and ethnic groups should be used. Avoid board books that have more than one idea or concept on a page, have a lot of text, or contain activities out of the realm of the baby's world. They should introduce families, food, or getting dressed, or objects such as toys, animals, cars, trucks, airplanes, or objects one sees in the home. Books showing one object per page are often called point-and-name books—the caregiver can point at the object and name it. Later the baby can point to the object, and when the baby can talk, the caregiver can point to the object and have the toddler name it. The caregiver can also extend text in a point-and-name book by saying, "You drink out of a cup, just like that." Often ABC books and counting books can be used as point-and-name books but should not be used to teach these academic skills. Plastic books are also a possibility, but one should avoid books that can float or be put in water. A baby needs to learn that a book is to be read and that a toy that floats in water is a totally different object! Cloth books are also a possibility, but cardboard books overall are better when children are between 16 and 18 months old. At this age they can help turn pages and hold the book, a difficult thing for young children to do when a book is made of cloth. Books that can be touched or have interesting textures are very good choices during this stage, as are manipulative books such as flap books or books with holes. Also good choices are books that contain rhymes, rhythm, repetition, or sounds.

Caregivers should talk and sing to their babies from infancy. Infants look at the person speaking to them and react to loud and soft sounds or voices. As mentioned earlier, simple hand, foot, and finger games are good, such as "Peek-a-Boo," "Pat-a-Cake," "Trot Trot to Boston," and "This Little Piggy," in addition to lap games where the infant is lifted and jostled. Because rhyme and rhythm are so important, Mother Goose nursery rhymes should be chanted, and lullabies and nursery songs sung. Remember that when children are between 12 to 18 months, they may imitate sounds or sing some words in nursery rhymes. It is also good for babies to hear different kinds of music on instruments, cassettes, compact discs, or the radio, and when old enough to stand, the children will sing and dance by moving their body to the music.

Caregivers also may want to make their own object books and touch-and-feel books with old magazines, catalogs, or materials around the home.

18 TO 30 MONTHS

DEVELOPMENTAL CHARACTERISTICS

Children are very active and seem to have boundless energy during this stage. They are curious about the world around them, always experimenting and testing, which is the reason why they learn so quickly. They are both imaginative and enthusiastic, also impatient and unpredictable. They are still very dependent on an adult caregiver and like to have the caregiver near them, but they also become assertive and independent at times, striving for autonomy. Many people unfortunately call this period of mood swings and temper tantrums "the terrible twos" because children are unafraid to say "no," will act negative at times, and often try to seek attention. But this assertiveness and testing of limits is important for children's later emotional makeup and the establishment of social skills. Being egocentric, they focus completely on themselves and believe that the world revolves around them. They take much pride in personal accomplishments and begin to understand the difference between right and wrong. The concept of sharing is not natural at this age; in fact, two-year-olds will often take toys away from others and not give them back even if the other child is screaming. During this time, children usually will not play with other children. Their play is either solitary or parallel; the latter means that a child will play next to, but independent of, another child. They also will not want to cooperate in group games. They are very observant, however, watching others to see how they do things and then imitating them. Fantasy play begins during this stage, with the toddler pretending to be someone or something else. They are also aware of their feelings and the feelings of others. The child is very trusting of the caregiver or person of authority, but also begins expressing fears of strangers, the dark, monsters, and sometimes animals.

Intellectually, the child has a very limited attention span. Curiosity, experimentation, and activity work against a longer attention span. Language is increasing with the child reaching a 200- to 800-word vocabulary by 30 months of age. Sentences are still short, however, normally around three words, such as "Me go too," or "Michelle go too." Some children will be able to call themselves by name. It is important that adults not use baby talk, but rather rich language that is not too complex. The child will follow simple directions and can answer yes-no questions. Simple concepts such as big and little, up and down, and loud and soft are understood. The difference between one and many is understood. Common objects, such as dog or cat, can be named. A two-year-old will know the difference between a boy and girl and can identify basic body parts. Memory is also developing.

Fine and gross motor skills are also increasing. The child can turn pages of a book one at a time and can name simple colors. The child can use large crayons, but is not good at coloring in the lines of a coloring book. Coloring is still scribbling, usually with horizontal or vertical strokes, though many children can draw a circle shape and will attempt drawing faces. The child can roll or squeeze clay, cut with blunt scissors, and paint with a large brush. Usually the whole arm is used to paint or color. Simple finger games are possible, but the child is incapable of holding one finger down at a time or three fingers up and two down. When looking for finger games, find those that have the child opening and closing the entire hand or pointing to fingers. The child enjoys stacking and working with blocks and can thread large beads on string. Easy toys can be taken apart and put back together. The child is very active and enjoys running, jumping, and kicking. In music, the child can sing or hum easy songs and enjoys songs with repetition. Also, the two-year-old enjoys clapping or marching to music.

IMPLICATIONS FOR BOOK SHARING AND ACTIVITIES

Nursery rhymes, songs, and poems should still be used. Heavy cardboard books with familiar objects and places are still a good choice, but if the child has been read to from infancy, books with paper pages can be used. Share simple, short stories with bright colors depicting objects in the child's realm of thought and with one concept or thought per page. A caregiver should encourage simple talk when reading books and the child will begin to ask questions. Have the child help act out or dramatize a part of the story if possible. The child may clap along with a rhythmic story or make a recurring sound in the story, for at this age, a child likes to imitate words or phrases. Children learn by participating. They are also developing a sense of humor and may appreciate easy books with funny situations they will understand. Stories about families, animals, or very easy folk tales are good choices.

Easy concept books that show relationships such as big and little or up and down are good choices. So are books that contain sounds, recurring words, rhythm, or rhyme. Books that provide tactile experiences should still be used. Choose books where a child can lift a flap, touch a surface, or look through a hole, such as in a peek-a-boo book, or poke their finger through a hole, as in a finger-wiggle book. Easy finger-game books that demonstrate one finger game per page are useful, as are nursery-rhyme or other song books designed for young children. Share easy information books such as color-concept books, counting or alphabet books, but again, read them for enjoyment rather than to teach academic skills. Use a variety of books, from small books children can carry in their hands to large books suitable for lap reading. Children can help turn the pages of the book and may wish to choose the book being read. Reading several short books several different times of the day is beneficial due to children's limited attention span.

Simple manipulative books can be made where a child can, for instance, zip a zipper or open and close a pocket. Also, easy puzzles can be made by cutting pieces from magazines, catalogs, or coloring books that depict one large object on a page, and mounting the pieces on cardboard. Puzzles should only be three or four pieces. Provide large pieces of paper, large crayons, finger paints, large brushes for paint, blunt scissors, play dough, and opportunities to play in water and in sand. Prepare for a messy environment!

A variety of songs and music should be used. Children may join in singing certain words or sounds and love to imitate. They will sway, bend, and move to the music. A puppet can be used to sing along, but remember, at this age, the child will probably think the puppet is alive!

2½ TO 3½ YEARS

DEVELOPMENTAL CHARACTERISTICS

Children between the ages of 2½ to 3½ are often very alike developmentally, which is why they are grouped together here.

Still very active, the older toddler has trouble sitting for a long period of time or listening quietly. The child prefers to be up and moving, with curiosity and exploration in the forefront. The older toddler continues to use senses of touch, smell, and taste to explore. Becoming more cooperative, parallel play eventually gives way to play with a small group of children. Sharing continues to be difficult, though it may occur with a sibling or a close friend. Taking turns is somewhat easier. The child strives for more independence and likes to do things alone, enjoying the feelings of accomplishment. This striving for identity is balanced by the need for security. A fear of separation, the dark, and strangers persists. Emotional swings are still apparent, and the child may become frustrated easily, though behavior is better controlled. Overall, thinking and behavior is still egocentric and the child's attention span remains short. The older toddler is rapidly acquiring language and may have a 1,200- to 1,500-word vocabulary by the age of 3½. Conversations are simple, with three- to six-word sentences, though the child learns to use some adverbs, verbs, pronouns, and prepositions correctly. Memory is improving, and by the age of three, some children can recite simple songs and rhymes or finger plays of four lines. Questions such as "why?" "what?" "where?" "when?"and "how?" become more common. Simple directions can be accurately followed.

Intellectual skills also are increasing. The child can understand more concepts, including simple science concepts and opposites such as happy and sad. The child can match common shapes and colors, identify ordinary animals, and name large and small body parts. Objects around the house, such as pieces of clothing, can be named and related objects paired. Children can help dress and undress themselves and are aware of sexual differences. Listening skills are also developing.

Hand-eye and small muscle coordination is difficult for a three-year-old child. Buttoning clothing can be a chore. However, fine motor skills are improving. Scribbling is still horizontal or vertical lines, but the child can copy a circle and attempt a straight line. People the child draws usually have a face and stick arms and legs. Coloring within lines is difficult for children at this age, but they begin to hold the crayon with their fingers rather than their fists. Painting should still be done with a large brush, and the child can now paste paper using a finger. Balls and snakes are made out of clay. The use of blunt scissors is more common, but the three-year-old is not good at cutting on lines and should not be expected to cut out figures or shapes. The child can sort objects into two categories, such as by color or shape. Finger games are easier for these children at this age because they can effortlessly close their fists and wiggle their fingers and thumbs.

Gross motor skills also are improving. The child enjoys running, climbing easy playground equipment, jumping, catching, and throwing. Balancing on one foot is possible. The child can master riding a tricycle at this age.

IMPLICATIONS FOR BOOK SHARING AND ACTIVITIES

Regular books with paper pages can now be read. Stories should be simple, with uncomplicated plots, and depict characters of various ages and ethnic groups that reflect the child's world. Children will enjoy looking at books on their own, and books should be kept in easy reach of the young child. Texts with rhyme, repetition, and silly or nonsense language should be used, along with participation stories where the child can repeat a line or make a sound. Plots that talk about dressing or feeding oneself and show other typical activities for this age group are popular. Simple counting rhymes, poems, and songs are excellent choices, along with books that provide opportunities for guessing. Other good choices are easy concept or informational books. Some stories can be presented using a flannel or magnetic board. Stories easily acted out, such as "The Three Bears," or ones in which the child can participate in dramatic play by imitating an animal or object will appeal to the child's sense of imagination. Make-believe is fun at this age and simple props or dress-up clothes will add to the fun. Children of this age can participate in group activities such as story-times, though they may be wary of participating at first and most will want a caregiver close by.

Caregivers will want to continue singing songs with the child and provide recordings the child can sing along with, listen to, and use along with movement. For example, "Ring Around the Rosie,"

"London Bridge," "Farmer in the Dell," and "If You're Happy and You Know It" are simple circle and movement games the young child will participate in. Three-year-olds can learn tunes and words to easy songs. They can recognize and imitate basic melodies, moving their body in rhythm to the music. Easy-to-play rhythm instruments can be purchased or made from household materials. Art materials such as large paper, crayons, large paint brushes, finger paints, marking pens, clay, chalk, and blunt scissors should be provided, along with opportunities for water and sand play. Young children can be asked to dictate a story or greeting in a card or letter to be mailed to other family members.

3½ THROUGH FIVE YEARS

DEVELOPMENTAL CHARACTERISTICS

Children are more independent and outgoing. They are still egocentric and also more assertive, confident, and self-assured. Usually the child has established a good self-identity and strives for independence from adults. They like to be around others of their own age and begin making friends. Play with small groups of children is more common and play is now often cooperative, rather than solitary. Children during this stage try to seek acceptance from their friends and often exclude children they do not like. They know right from wrong, seeking justice for wrong actions or behavior, and rewards for good behavior or actions. Sharing is much easier. Activity could best be described as exuberant during the fourth year, but somewhat more peaceful by age five. Children often become more bossy and boastful, but attention span has also increased. Senses and memory are more developed. Curiosity is still present and the questions "why?" "when?" "how?" and "what?" continue.

The vocabulary of the average four- and five-year-old will range from 1,200 words to 2,500 or more words by the fifth year. Children will become much more talkative during this stage and are unafraid to be noisy. Sentences contain from five to ten words and are more grammatically correct. Children find playing with words and making up new silly words fun. Five-year-olds can usually count to 20, list the days of the week, and identify some letters, first learning those in their name. By the age of five, children can begin to recognize some words of print in a book, their names, and also environmental print such as traffic signs or cereal boxes.

Writing skills also have increased. Children by the age of four or five will begin to copy their names and can begin to write numbers up to ten and some letters of the alphabet. The child is better equipped to name objects and colors, and by the age of five can compare objects by color, size, and shape. The child's listening skills have increased, as has the ability to follow directions. Also expanding is the child's interest in learning. Often children can name and tell the function of various body parts and can give vital information about themselves such as their name, address, phone number, and age.

Fine motor skills are more developed. By the end of the fourth year, the child can use scissors to cut on a straight line. Left-handedness or right-handedness is usually apparent by the age of five. When drawing a human figure, the child can add approximately six body parts, such as the head, arms, legs, and some facial features. At age five, the child can trace patterns within a square page, color within lines, and copy letters or shapes. The child often reverses letters at this time, however, though this should not be a concern. Dressing (including buttoning and buckling) is usually a snap by age four. Simple puzzles of ten or more pieces and games such as connect-the-dots are possible during the latter part of this stage. Jigsaw puzzles, construction toys, blocks, and peg boards are popular.

Gross motor skills progress as the child skips, hops, climbs, gallops, jumps from heights, rides a tricycle and then a bicycle (first with training wheels), and climbs on outdoor play equipment. The child can clap and march to music, respond to a steady rhythm, and participate in group singing.

IMPLICATIONS FOR BOOK SHARING AND ACTIVITIES

Children will enjoy a variety of books, not only of different types and with a variety of illustrations, but also of varying lengths, with more detail and description. Plots can be more complex and subject matter can not only relate to everyday life but also be adventurous or silly. Books about dinosaurs, monsters, giants, and machinery, or easy fact books are popular with four- and five-year-olds. Choose different types of books: participation, cumulative, repetitious, rhyme, humorous, nonsense, fairy tales, folk tales, concepts, riddles, poetry, and fantasy. Children enjoy make-believe during this time, and some have imaginary friends and engage in imaginative play. During this stage, children also engage in sociodramatic play, which is make-believe play, shared or coordinated with another child. Imaginative play revolves around superheroes, fierce animals or monsters, or book or television characters. Encourage imaginative play with the use of creative dramatics and puppetry. Often children will act out the story or have the puppet tell part of the story without any adult modeling.

It is good to introduce a variety of methods of storytelling for children of these ages. Use clothesline stories, with each child receiving a character to be hung on the clothesline at a particular time, or magnetic or flannel-board stories, allowing the children to place the figures on the board at the appropriate time. Both of these methods allow the children to participate and become involved in the story. Children can also retell folk tales and at the age of four or five can make up stories that go with wordless books by just observing the pictures closely. Puppetry is also important for imaginative play and homemade puppets can be just as popular as store-bought ones.

Children will often want the same stories read over and over. As trying as that might seem to caregivers, it is actually good to do. Children will begin to memorize the story and can often retell it. They will also sometimes take the book by themselves and pretend to read it. By five years of age, they will show an interest in print and will begin to recognize words or letters by sight. Some five-year-olds will begin to read independently. Caregivers should write stories that children dictate and have the children draw pictures. Some children will even attempt to write the words and caregivers should not correct their invented spelling.

Often parents will drill their children to learn ABCs, numbers, and phonics, which is not usually a good idea. This type of learning is rote and means little because the child does not really understand the information. It is better that parents introduce their child to a print-rich environment by reading, providing magnetic letters to play with, and having the child dictate stories or letters. Academic skills should not be emphasized, nor should the use of preschool workbooks or dittos sheets be encouraged. Children should be allowed to explore and experience things and will learn by doing creative activities.

Children should be exposed to various forms and types of music. They can keep time to the music and will enjoy singing songs with a group of children and clapping and marching. Rhythm instruments are very appealing. Finger plays are no longer a problem and children have the fine motor skills to perform different types. Dramatic play and role-playing should be encouraged. Include props and dress-up clothing.

Art activities should be varied also. At this age, children will be able to draw specific items they know in their lives. Paper, pencils, pens, crayons, markers, chalk, scissors, finger paints, and clay should be provided. By the age of five, the child can work with collages, watercolors, and tempera paint. Provide opportunities for children to do their own creative art, rather than coloring pages. Stencils or cardboard cut-outs to trace and color will provide fine motor practice. Children should be encouraged to engage in their own arts and crafts, rather than copying adult-made models.

SIX THROUGH EIGHT YEARS

DEVELOPMENTAL CHARACTERISTICS

Six- through eight-year-old children are very active physically and prefer hands-on activities that are active rather than passive. Play is cooperative and usually with friends of the same sex. Peer groups become important during these ages. Children will visit and play with friends independent of adult supervision and are very self-sufficient. Self-esteem is usually high and children feel competent. They will often show possessiveness of belongings and friends. Emotionally, the child can be assertive, even argumentative and stubborn with others. The child may have difficulty listening to a caregiver and may question the caregiver's authority, but still craves attention and affection from the caregiver. Children become very competitive during this stage and have a desire to be first, which also leads to boasting. They are more in control of their emotions now and less egocentric than when they were younger. There is a clear sense of actions being either all good or all bad, which means children believe in obeying rules and will tattletale if another child does an action the first child considers bad.

The child has a much longer attention span and can sit still for a much longer period of time. Intellectually, there is much advancement. At age six, the child can recognize letters and words in books and will eventually learn to read. The child can read independently fairly soon and often enjoys showing off reading skills. There is a wide variation in reading abilities of children during this stage with some children reading "I can read" books for some time, while others advance quickly to chapter books, with chapters they can read in one sitting.

Because children of this age are now involved in a formal learning situation, they are often very eager to learn. Vocabulary has increased to over 6,000 words and sentences become more complex. Children have a sense of time and concepts are developed. Problem-solving ability improves.

By age six, children will establish using their left or right hand, and eye-hand coordination improves. Writing skills also increase and children show much pride in their writing. At first, children may reverse letters and will spell words incorrectly, but caregivers should allow inventive spelling at first, rather than discourage the child from writing. They can print neatly and copy complex figures by the age of seven. Children no longer need to cut on a straight line but can cut angular shapes. Crafts, hobbies, and collections are often begun and many children begin playing musical instruments.

Gross motor skills are almost completely developed during this time. Children can ride bicycles, skip, hop, climb, play ball, play active games, play sports, and are often in motion!

IMPLICATIONS FOR BOOK SHARING AND ACTIVITIES

Though children learn to read independently during this time, it is crucial that caregivers and teachers still read aloud to them. It is just as important for children to have the desire to read as it is for them to learn how to read. Obtaining a desire to read is often acquired by having others read to them and by seeing adults read for pleasure. Adults should read books to children at a more advanced level, since the children's interest will be at a different level than their reading abilities. Caregivers may use longer-chapter books, but should continue to read picture books to the child, because the variety of art in these books leads the child to a greater appreciation of art. Older children can also participate by reading to their younger siblings or children of this age may read to each other. Children will be at different reading levels and should not be forced to read at any one grade level.

Books read should comprise a variety of subjects, lengths, and complexities. Various types of stories should be shared: realistic, fantasy, humorous, dramatic, family, school, tall tales, sports, multicultural, and wordless (have the child tell the story). Easy information or fact books are good choices, along with riddle and joke books, craft or hobby books, game books, and the like. Children should be able to select some of the books read to them. Quality films or videos of children's books can also be viewed.

Writing should also be encouraged. Though children soon will be able to write their own cards or letters, they should still have the chance to dictate stories during the early part of this stage. When children are seven or eight, they can begin to write or illustrate their own books. Riddle or joke books, family stories, stories about book characters, or stories that revolve around holidays will be particularly enjoyable.

A variety of forms of music and movement should be employed, with children learning how to play instruments or appreciating recordings. Art activities also should vary, with children doing their own creative work, rather than copying adult-made models.

SIMPLIFIED DEVELOPMENT CHARTS

Following are simplified charts of developmental characteristics of young children by stages and implications for book sharing and activities. Suggested appropriate books for young children's developmental stages are also appended.

FIGURE 2.1 Simplified Developmental Charts

Birth to 18 Months
Simplified Chart

DEVELOPMENTAL CHARACTERISTICS

Of Infants:
• Discriminate primary colors, though not shades of color
• Are attracted to patterns that show high contrasts between dark and light (such as black and white)
• Are fascinated by faces and things that move
• Respond to human voices and can differentiate voices
• Respond to music, sounds, and singing
• Babble and coo
• Like to be held and touched
• Like to touch, grasp, and suck objects
• Will smile and laugh by four months
• Will kick their legs, roll over, sit with support, and throw objects by six months
• Will creep and crawl and begin to pull themselves up by nine months
• Will walk with help, climb up stairs, drink from a cup, and wave goodbye by 10 or 11 months

Of 12- to 18-month old children:
• Understand many simple words and directions
• Imitate simple words, sounds, and actions
• Like songs and rhymes repeated
• Pick up objects and put them in and out of containers
• Are curious and like to watch other children
• Use telegraphic speech (two words [content words] like ''Mommy home'')
• Understand more words than they can speak
• Name familiar objects and basic body parts
• Develop simple memory

FIGURE 2.1 Continued

- Learn to walk around one year of age
- Rely on their senses by touching, smelling, or tasting objects
- Stack blocks and play with simple toys
- Scribble with crayons, either vertically or horizontally
- Help turn pages of a book
- Move or sway to music
- Attached to their caregiver but are somewhat assertive

SUGGESTIONS FOR BOOK SHARING AND ACTIVITIES

Infants

Books
- Use heavy cardboard books with round edges; also cloth books
- Choose books that depict bright colors and definite contrasts between light and dark
- Pictures should show familiar objects, one object per page; also faces
- Use point-and-name books
- Use books with textures that can be touched
- Share Mother Goose nursery rhymes

Activities
- Talk to, sing to, and read to the baby
- Use simple hand, feet and finger games such as "Peek-a-Boo," Pat-a-Cake," and "This Little Piggy"
- Use lap games, lifting and jostling the baby
- Sing lullabies and nursery songs
- Play different types of music (not just children's songs)
- Make homemade object or touch-and-feel books

12- to 18-month old children

Books
- Use heavy cardboard books with round edges
- Pictures should show familiar objects, one object per page, or uncluttered pictures
- Use point-and-name books
- Use books with textures that can be touched
- Use manipulative books, such as flap books or books with holes
- Use books with rhymes, rhythm, and repetition
- Use books where the child can imitate simple words, sounds, or actions
- Share Mother Goose nursery rhymes

Activities
- Talk to, sing to, and read to the child
- Use simple hand, feet and finger games such as "Peek-a-Boo," Pat-a-Cake," and "This Little Piggy"
- Sing lullabies and nursery songs and dance with the child
- Play different types of music (not just children's songs)
- Make homemade object or touch-and-feel books

FIGURE 2.1 Continued

18 Months to 30 Months (1½ to 2½ years)
Simplified Chart

DEVELOPMENTAL CHARACTERISTICS OF TODDLERS:
- Are very active
- Are curious about the world around them, experimenting and testing
- Are imaginative, enthusiastic, impatient, unpredictable
- Are dependent on a caregiver but also strive for autonomy
- Are not afraid to say no and be assertive
- Seek attention
- Are egocentric—the world revolves around them
- Take pride in personal accomplishments
- Begin to know the difference between right and wrong
- Do not want to share
- Engage in solitary play and later parallel play (play next to but not with other children)
- Observe others and imitate actions
- Begin fantasy or pretend play
- Are aware of their feelings and feelings of others
- Are trusting of the caregiver
- Develop fears of strangers, the dark, monsters, etc.
- Have a limited attention span
- Have a 200- to 800-word vocabulary by 30 months
- Say their name and speak three-word sentences
- Follow simple directions
- Understand easy concepts
- Name common objects and body parts
- Develop more memory
- Turn pages of a book
- Name basic colors
- Scribble horizontal or vertical strokes; can also draw a circle and simple faces
- Use large crayons and paint brush; roll, pound, or squeeze clay; use blunt scissors
- Use their whole arm to paint or color
- Are capable of simple finger games
- Stack blocks and thread large beads
- Enjoy running, jumping, and kicking
- Sing or hum to music and enjoy songs with repetition
- Clap, bend, sway, or march to music

SUGGESTIONS FOR BOOK SHARING AND ACTIVITIES

Books
- Use heavy cardboard books until books with paper pages can be shared
- Read simple, short books several times a day, due to limited attention span
- Select books with bright colors with subjects familiar to the child's environment

FIGURE 2.1 Continued

- Share a variety of books with different sizes, shapes, etc.
- Choose books about families, animals, funny situations, simple folk tales, or basic concepts
- Pick texts that contain sounds, recurring words, rhythm, or rhyme
- Furnish books that provide tactile experiences such as flaps to raise; surfaces to touch; finger holes to poke fingers through; or peek-a-boo books (books with circles or shapes cut out of a page that child can peek through)
- Read easy information books such as color, ABC, and counting books, but not to teach academic skills
- Encourage the child to participate by talking, making sounds, or acting out the story
- Have the child help turn the pages and select books to be read
- Make homemade books such as manipulative books; also easy puzzles with three to four pieces

Activities
- Share nursery rhymes, songs, poems, and finger plays
- Provide large pieces of paper, large crayons, finger paints, large paint brushes, blunt scissors, clay
- Allow much water and sand play
- Use a variety of songs and music (not just children's music)
- Have the child sing some words or make sounds during songs
- Encourage the toddler to imitate actions/words
- Use puppets, but remember children will probably think they are alive

2½ Years to 3½ Years
Simplified Chart

DEVELOPMENTAL CHARACTERISTICS OF TODDLERS:
- Are very active and do not sit still long or quietly
- Are very curious and like to explore and use their senses
- Are more cooperative—parallel play leads to play with a small group of children
- Have trouble sharing though they may with a sibling or close friend
- Begin taking turns with other children
- Strive for independence but still have a need for security
- Enjoy feelings of accomplishment
- Fear separation, dark, and strangers
- Have emotional swings (they frustrate easily though they control behavior better)
- Are still egocentric
- Have a short attention span
- Have a 1,200- to 1,500-word vocabulary possible by the age of 3½
- Use three- to six-word sentences
- Start to use adverbs, verbs, pronouns, and prepositions correctly
- Have improved memory and can recite songs and rhymes of four lines
- Ask constant questions—why, what, where, when, how
- Follow simple directions
- Understand more concepts, including easy science concepts
- Match common shapes and colors
- Identify animals and objects around the house or in the environment
- Name large and small body parts

FIGURE 2.1 Continued

- Help dress and undress themselves
- Are aware of sexual differences
- Have difficulty with eye-hand and small muscle coordination
- Scribble horizontal or vertical lines
- Copy a circle and attempt straight lines
- Draw people with a face and stick arms and legs
- Hold crayons with fingers rather than with fists (still hard to color within lines)
- Paint with a large brush and paste paper with their fingers
- Make clay balls and snakes
- Use blunt scissors but are not good at cutting on lines
- Sort objects by color and shape
- Perform simple finger games
- Enjoy running, climbing, jumping, catching, and throwing
- Balance on one foot
- Ride tricycles

SUGGESTIONS FOR BOOK SHARING AND ACTIVITIES

Books

Adult:
- Share books with paper pages
- Read books with simple, uncomplicated plots depicting characters of various ages and ethnic groups
- Use participation stories and stories with rhyme, repetition and silly language
- Read stories that show typical activities like dressing and feeding oneself
- Share books with counting rhymes, poems, songs and simple guessing games
- Read easy concept or informational books
- Use flannel or magnetic board presentations
- Have the child act out stories or imitate animals or objects in the book
- Extend stories with simple props or dress-up clothes

Child:
- Will look at books on their own if kept in easy reach
- Can tell the story from the pictures

Activities

Adult:
- Continue singing songs with the child
- Provide recordings of different types of music the child can sing or move to
- Provide large paper, crayons, large paint brushes, finger paints, marking pens, clay, chalk and blunt scissors
- Allow time for water and sand play
- Have child dictate stories or messages for greeting cards, letters, etc.

Child:
- Carries a tune and learns easy words to songs
- Recognizes and imitates simple melodies

FIGURE 2.1 Continued

- Moves body in rhythm to music
- Recites easy poems and rhymes
- Plays easy-to-use rhythm instruments
- Participates in simple circle and movement games
- Participates in group activities like storytimes

3½ Years Through 5 Years
Simplified Chart

DEVELOPMENTAL CHARACTERISTICS OF PRESCHOOLERS
- Are still egocentric
- Are more independent, assertive, confident, and self-assured (good self-identity)
- Make friends with others of the same age and seek acceptance by these friends
- Participate in cooperative play with small groups of children
- Know right from wrong—expect rewards for good behavior and punishment for wrong actions
- Begin sharing
- Are exuberant at age four but activity is somewhat more controlled by age five
- Boast and are bossy
- Have an increasing interest span and can sit for a longer period of time listening
- Have memory and senses developing at a faster rate
- Are very curious and enjoy learning
- Ask many why, when, how and what questions
- Have a 1,200 to 2,500 or more word vocabulary by age five
- Are more talkative and noisy
- Speak sentences of five to ten words that are more grammatically correct with tenses used properly
- Play with and make up words
- Count to 20
- Identify some letters, first learning their name
- Recognize environmental print and some words in books at age five
- Copy their name, write numbers up to ten, write some letters and simple words
- Compare objects by color, size, and shape, naming common shapes by age five
- Listen better and increase their ability to follow directions
- Name and tell functions of various body parts
- Give their name, phone number, and age
- Use scissors with control and can cut on a straight line
- Develop left-handedness or right-handedness, usually apparent by age five
- Draw human figures adding at least six major body parts
- Trace patterns that are within pages accurately
- Color within lines and copy letters or shapes
- Learn to zip, button, buckle, and lace when dressing
- Like puzzles of ten or more pieces, easy connect-the-dots, construction toys, blocks, and peg boards
- Skip, hop, climb, jump, ride a tricycle and then a bicycle with training wheels
- Clap and march to music, respond to a beat, participate in group singing

FIGURE 2.1 Continued

SUGGESTIONS FOR BOOK SHARING AND ACTIVITIES

Books

Adult:
- Read a variety of books with more detail and description
- Plots can be more complex—about everyday life, adventure or fantasy
- Share: participation, cumulative, repetitious, rhymed, humorous, nonsense, fairy-tale, folk-tale, concept, riddle, poetry, and make-believe books
- Introduce a variety of storytelling methods: magnetic or flannelboard stories, clothesline stories, participation stories, creative dramatics, and puppetry

Child:
- Memorizes stories such as folk tales and retells them
- Recites songs and poems from memory
- Makes up stories to go with wordless books
- Likes stories repeated
- Pretends to read books
- Has interest in print—recognizes some words or letters by sight
- Some children may read independently by age five

Activities

Adult:
- Encourage imaginative play by using creative dramatics, puppetry, dress-up clothing, and props
- Do not drill the child in ABCs, numbers, phonics, or workbook or ditto sheets
- Introduce a print-rich environment: read to them; have magnetic letters to play with; have them dictate stories and see print; and have them help make books
- Expose them to various forms and types of music
- Provide varied art materials—paper, pencils, pens, crayons, markers, chalk, clay, scissors, fingerpaints
- Engage children in their own creative art, rather than copying adult-made models

Child:
- Has imaginary friends and engages in imaginative play which revolves around superheroes, fierce animals, monsters, book or TV characters
- Engages in sociodramatic play (make-believe play shared with another)
- Should dictate stories to adults and illustrate them
- Begins to write and uses invented spelling (which should not be corrected)
- Keeps time to music, sings songs with a group of children, enjoys silly songs and echo songs, claps and marches to music
- Finds rhythm instruments appealing
- Finger plays and circle and movement games are still important
- Capable of independently working in collage, watercolors, and tempera paint

FIGURE 2.1 Continued

6 Years Through 8 Years
Simplified Chart

DEVELOPMENTAL CHARACTERISTICS OF CHILDREN:
- Are very active physically
- Prefer hands-on activities that are active, rather than passive
- Participate in cooperative play—usually with friends of the same sex
- Find peer groups important
- Visit and play with friends independently
- Have high self-esteem generally
- Are possessive of belongings and friends
- May be assertive, argumentative, and stubborn with others
- May question an adult's authority and have difficulty listening
- Crave attention and affection from the caregiver
- Like to compete and desire to be first
- Are less egocentric and more in control of their emotions
- Believe all actions are either good or bad and will tattletale on other children
- Have a longer attention span and can sit for a longer period of time
- Learn to read, acquiring a larger vocabulary each year (over 6,000 words)
- Have a wide variation of reading abilities among this age group
- Are eager to learn
- Use more complex sentences
- Improve in problem-solving ability
- Establish left-handedness or right-handedness
- Improve their eye-hand coordination
- Increase their writing skills though they may reverse letters and spell words incorrectly
- Print neatly and copy complex figures by the age of seven
- Like crafts, hobbies, and collections
- May begin playing musical instruments
- Have well-developed gross motor skills
- Enjoy active games, sports, and riding bicycles

SUGGESTIONS FOR BOOK SHARING AND ACTIVITIES

Books

Adult:
- Should continue to read books to the child at a more advanced reading level even though the child is reading independently
- Select books with a variety of subjects, lengths, and complexity
- Share quality films or videos of children's books

Child:
- Begins to read independently
- Should read to other siblings or friends
- Enjoys books about games, crafts, hobbies, jokes, riddles, magic, silly poetry, fantasy and real-life stories

FIGURE 2.1 Continued

- Loves to show off reading skills
- Likes to select books on their own for reading

Activities

Adult:

- Encourage independent writing but also have child dictate messages or stories
- Should not drill child in ABCs, numbers, phonics, or workbook or ditto sheets
- Have children write, design, and illustrate their own books
- Expose children to a variety of forms of music and movement
- Have children learn how to play a musical instrument of their choice
- Encourage creative art activities with a variety of mediums
  (Do not have children copy adult-made models)

Appropriate Books for Young Children's Developmental Stages

The following bibliography is to be used as a guide only. This list is limited to 12 suggested titles for each stage, except for ages six to eight, which is noted below. There are many more excellent books that could be recommended. Consult the "Simplified Charts" of developmental characteristics to pick books appropriate for each stage. It is also suggested you consult the bibliography of "Resource Books on Reading Aloud to Children" contained in Chapter 3 for other selections (see Fig. 3.1).

Birth to 18 Months

Infants

Baum, Susan. *Animals for Baby*. New York: Harper Festival, 1993. Others included in the series: *Farm Friends; Things That Go;* and *Playtime for Baby*.

> These cloth books have bright colors, one familiar object per page and are good point-and-name books.

Chorao, Kay. *Baby's Lap Book*. New York: Dutton, 1991.

> A book and cassette of Mother Goose rhymes. There are several excellent Mother Goose books. Pick one you like with illustrations that will attract a baby. *The Real Mother Goose* by Blanche Wright is also available as several board books.

Cole, Joanna, and Stephanie Calmenson, comps. *Pat-A-Cake and Other Play Rhymes*. New York: Morrow Junior, 1992.

> Simple hand, feet, and finger games to play with baby.

Cousins, Lucy. *Teddy in the House*. Cambridge: Candlewick Press, 1992. Others included in the series: *Hen on the Farm; Flower in the Garden;* and *Kite in the Park*.

> These cloth books have bright colors with definite contrasts and one familiar object per page. They are useful as point-and-name books.

Davies, Kate. *Patterns*. New York: Grosset & Dunlap, 1993. Also, *Pictures*.

> Both are cloth "Baby Bumper Books" with black and white images. *Pictures* shows familiar objects including a face. The point-and-name books contain just one object per page.

FIGURE 2.1 Continued

Foord, Jo. *The Book of Babies: A First Picture Book of All the Things That Babies Do.* New York: Random, 1991. Henderson, Kathy. *The Baby's Book of Babies.* New York: Dial, 1989.

Two books depicting large photos of multi-ethnic babies and baby faces. With Foord's book, you do not need to read the entire text for infants, just read the one large word given on each page.

Hill, Eric. *Clothes.* New York: Putnam, 1993. Others included in the series: *Animals; Home;* and *Play.*

These cloth books employ primary colors and familiar objects and are useful as point-and-name books. The popular puppy Spot appears in each book.

Hoban, Tana. *White on Black.* New York: Greenwillow, 1993. Also, *Black on White.*

Two cardboard books with rounded edges that present high contrast between black and white objects. Familiar objects are shown, one object per page, which make good point-and-name books. Two other excellent high contrast books done in black and white and with colorful borders are *Let's Look at Animals* and *Let's Look at My World* illustrated by Dick Witt and published by Scholastic in 1993.

Ra, Carol, comp. *Trot, Trot to Boston.* New York: Lothrop, Lee & Shepard Books, 1987.

Rhymes to play with baby where the infant is touched or jostled. Notes with actions are included.

Wattenberg, Jane. *Mrs. Mustard's Baby Faces.* San Francisco: Chronicle, 1989.

Photos of multi-ethnic baby faces of happy and not-so-happy babies are depicted on a patterned background. Infants are attracted to faces.

Williams, Sarah, comp. *Ride a Cock-Horse.* Oxford: Oxford University Press, 1986.

Rhymes that babies can be bounced, touched, jostled, or sung to, with notes on actions.

Yolen, Jane, ed. *The Lap-Time Song and Play Book.* San Diego: Harcourt Brace, 1989.

Lap games and songs to lift, touch and jostle baby with notes on actions to be performed.

12 to 18 Months

Cousins, Lucy. *Pet Animals.* New York: Tambourine, 1990. Others included in the series: *Country Animals; Farm Animals;* and *Garden Animals.*

These cardboard books with rounded edges and one object per page are to be used as point-and-name books.

Emerson, Sally, comp. *The Kingfisher Nursery Rhyme Songbook.* New York: Kingfisher, 1991. Barratt, Carol. *The Mother Goose Songbook.* New York: Derrydale Books, 1986. Glazer, Tom. *The Mother Goose Songbook.* New York: Doubleday, 1990. Glazer, Tom. *Music for Ones and Twos.* New York: Doubleday, 1983. Larrick, Nancy, comp. *Songs from Mother Goose.* New York: HarperCollins, 1989.

All contain familiar Mother Goose nursery rhyme songs with music.

Hill, Eric. *Where's Spot?* New York: Putnam, 1980.

A manipulative flap book in which the word "No" is repeated, inviting child participation.

Hoban, Tana. *Red, Blue, Yellow Shoe.* New York: Greenwillow, 1986. Also, *1,2,3* and *What Is It?*

These cardboard books with rounded edges and one object per page are to be used as point-and-name books.

Johnson, Audean. *Soft as a Kitten: Things to Touch and Feel, See and Sniff.* New York: Random, 1982.

A manipulative book to touch, feel, and smell.

FIGURE 2.1 Continued

Kemp, Moira, illus. *This Little Piggy.* New York: Lodestar, 1990. Others included in the series: *Hey Diddle Diddle; Hickory Dickory, Dock;* and *Baa, Baa, Black Sheep.*

Each cardboard book with rounded edges is an individual nursery rhyme.

Leslie, Amanda. *Play Kitten Play.* Cambridge: Candlewick Press, 1992. Also, *Play Puppy Play.*

These cardboard books with rounded edges have holes (fingerwiggles) for children to stick their fingers through.

Oxenbury, Helen. *All Fall Down.* New York: Macmillan, 1987. Also: *Clap Hands; Say Goodnight;* and *Tickle, Tickle.* Morris, Ann. *This Little Baby's Bedtime.* Boston: Little, Brown, 1993. Others included in the series: *This Little Baby Goes Out; This Little Baby's Morning;* and *This Little Baby's Playtime.*

All are cardboard books with rounded edges depicting toddlers of various races interacting with each other and their parents.

Patterson, Bettina. *My Clothes.* New York: Henry Holt, 1992. Others included in the series: *In My House; In My Yard;* and *My Toys.*

These cardboard books with rounded edges, bright colors, and one familiar object per page can be used as point-and-name books.

Shott, Stephen, photographer. *Look at Me.* New York: Dutton, 1991. Others included in the "Look At Me Book" series: *Bathtime; Mealtime;* and *Playtime.*

This cardboard book with rounded edges is illustrated with photos of babies at this age. The child can imitate the actions and follow the simple directions given.

Tafuri, Nancy. *One Wet Jacket.* New York: Greenwillow, 1988. Also: *In a Red House; My Friends; Two New Sneakers;* and *Where We Sleep.*

All are cardboard books with rounded edges, bright colors, familiar objects and one object per page to be used as point-and-name books. Each page contains one word in large print.

Williams, Sarah, comp. *Round and Round the Garden.* Oxford: Oxford University Press, 1983. Also, *Ride a Cock-Horse.*

Play rhymes with motions and movements given on the bottom of the page are accompanied by bright colored illustrations.

18 Months to 30 Months (1½ Years to 2½ Years)

Brown, Margaret Wise. *Goodnight Moon.* New York: HarperCollins, 1947. Also board book version, 1993.

Recurring words, familiar objects, and a reassuring rhyme encourage the child to participate.

Carle, Eric. *The Very Busy Spider.* New York: Philomel, 1984.

The child can participate by making sounds and by touching the raised relief spider web.

Carter, Noelle. *My Pet.* New York: Viking, 1991. Also, *My House.*

There are animals to name, pop-ups and flaps to manipulate, and bright colors in this series.

Carter, Noelle, and David Carter. *I'm a Little Mouse.* New York: Henry Holt, 1990.

With surfaces to touch and feel, and a chance for the child to participate and answer questions, this book depicting familiar animals is a good choice.

FIGURE 2.1 Continued

Cousins, Lucy. *What Can Rabbit Hear?* New York: Tambourine, 1991. Also, *What Can Rabbit See?*

There are bright colors, flaps to lift, and opportunities for the child to participate and answer questions. Familiar animals, insects, and objects are used.

Duncan, Lois. *Songs from Dreamland.* New York: Knopf, 1989.

Original lullabies and poems with an accompanying cassette make this perfect for bedtime sharing.

Ehlert, Lois. *Fish Eyes.* San Diego: Harcourt Brace, 1990.

Bright colors are employed along with a simple counting concept and finger holes. When the child is older, the book can be used for simple math concepts.

Hayes, Sarah, comp. *Clap Your Hands: Finger Rhymes.* New York: Lothrop, Lee & Shepard, 1988. Also, *Stamp Your Feet: Action Rhymes.*

The child can participate in these simple finger and action rhymes since actions/motions are provided.

Jonas, Ann. *When You Were a Baby.* New York: Greenwillow, 1982.

A heavy cardboard book with rounded edges and bright colors tells children what they can do now that they are no longer a baby.

Martin, Bill. *Here Are My Hands.* New York: Henry Holt, 1985. Similar is: Hudson, Cheryl Willis, and Bernette G. Ford. *Bright Eyes, Brown Skin.* Orange, N.J.: Just Us Books, 1990.

The child can participate by pointing to each body part named. The texts have a rhythmic flow.

Rikys, Bodel. *Red Bear.* New York: Dial, 1992.

This basic color-concept book with bright colors and familiar objects is an appealing choice.

Young, Ruth. *Golden Bear.* New York: Viking, 1992.

This simple rhymed text accompanied by bright colored pictures allows the child to act out the actions described and may provide pretend play possibilities.

2½ Years to 3½ Years

Bang, Molly, *Ten, Nine, Eight.* New York: Greenwillow, 1983.

A good selection for bedtime with rhyme and a counting concept.

Browne, Jane. *Sing Me a Song.* New York: Crown, 1991.

Action songs, finger games, circle and movement games with illustrations depicting young children.

Campbell, Rod. *Dear Zoo.* New York: Four Winds, 1982.

There are flaps to raise in this simple guessing game that encourages verbal participation.

Crews, Donald. *Freight Train.* New York: Greenwillow, 1978.

A color-concept and informational book inviting participation and with the added appeal of a train.

Ehlert, Lois. *Planting a Rainbow.* San Diego: Harcourt Brace, 1988.

Easy science and color concepts are introduced in this book with bright colors.

Hale, Sarah J. *Mary Had a Little Lamb.* New York: Scholastic, 1990.

The complete version of this rhyme is given with photographs depicting an African-American child. Children can sing along with the first verse of the song.

FIGURE 2.1 Continued

Lillie, Patricia. *Everything Has a Place.* New York: Greenwillow, 1993.

An easy concept book where the child can participate by identifying objects or by joining in the simple guessing game. Illustrations depict familiar objects in the environment and tell where they belong.

MacKinnon, Debbie. *What Shape?* New York: Dial, 1992. Similar is: Rikys, Bodel. *Red Bear's Fun with Shapes.* New York: Dial, 1993.

For both books, the child can match common shapes and colors. Bright colors are used. Children can trace shapes with their fingers. MacKinnon's book can be used as a point-and-name book.

Martin, Bill. *Brown Bear, Brown Bear, What Do You See?* New York: Henry Holt, 1992.

This popular color concept book provides rhyme, repetition, participation, and a simple guessing game.

Tafuri, Nancy. *Who's Counting?* New York: Greenwillow, 1986.

Bright colors are used in this counting concept, point-and-name book.

Watanabe, Shigeo. *How Do I Put It On?* New York: Philomel, 1984. Also: *What a Good Lunch?; I Can Take a Walk!;* and *Where's My Daddy?*

These books present typical activities like dressing and feeding oneself, which the child can now master. Simple participation is encouraged.

Zelinsky, Paul. *Wheels of the Bus.* New York: Dutton, 1990. Raffi. *Wheels of the Bus.* New York: Crown, 1988.

Both versions encourage the child to sing along and act out and use motions with the song. Zelinsky's version has tabs and flaps to pull.

3½ Years Through 5 Years

Aylesworth, Jim. *Old Black Fly.* New York: Henry Holt, 1992.

A great participation, rhyme, and ABC concept book that will be asked for again and again.

Brown, Marc. *Finger Rhymes.* New York: Dutton, 1980. Also: *Hand Rhymes; Party Rhymes;* and *Play Rhymes.*

Familiar rhymes are accompanied by motions.

Burton, Jane. *Kitten.* "See How They Grow" Series. New York: Lodestar, 1991. Numerous entries in this series including: Chick; Duck; Frog; Lamb; Mouse; Puppy; Rabbit, and many more.

Easy science concepts are provided in these informational books that satisfy curiosity and answer common questions.

Cole, Joanna. *Read Aloud Treasury.* Doubleday, 1988.

A collection of picture book stories, folk tales, poetry, and nursery rhymes.

Ehlert, Lois. *Color Zoo.* New York: J.B. Lippincott, 1989.

Ehlert uses bright, bold graphics for the child to identify objects by shape. As an art extension, have children make their own animals with common shapes.

Emberley, Ed. *Go Away, Big Green Monster!* Boston: Little, Brown, 1993.

Die-cut pages reveal a monster face piece by piece. This is designed to help children overcome their fear of monsters. Bright, colorful, and fun!

Glazer, Tom. *Eye Winker, Tom Tinker, Chin Chopper.* New York: Doubleday, 1973. Beall, Pamela C., and Nipp, Susan H. *Wee Sing.* Los Angeles: Price/Stern/Sloan, 1981. (A series with many other titles.)

Musical fingerplays with music and motions supplied.

FIGURE 2.1 Continued

Guarino, Deborah. *Is Your Mama a Llama?* New York: Scholastic, 1989.

A riddle book with rhyme and humor that invites participation.

Hopkins, Lee Bennett, collector. *Side by Side.* New York: Simon & Schuster, 1988.

A poetry collection ideal for sharing with young children.

Martin, Bill. *Chicka Chicka Boom Boom.* New York: Simon & Schuster, 1988.

Another popular choice with rhyme, rhythm, and participation and that can be used for letter identification.

Rosen, Michael. *We're Going on a Bear Hunt.* New York: McElderry, 1989.

This familiar, humorous tale elicits participation and is great for creative dramatics.

Young, Ed. *Seven Blind Mice.* New York: Philomel, 1992.

Based on a fable from India, this tale introduces the concepts of color identification, ordinal numbers, and days of the week.

6 Years Through 8 Years

Books To Share With Six- To Eight-Year-Old Children

The list of good books that can be shared with this age group, as with the other groups, is long indeed. To limit the list to 12 suggested titles, as above, would be very difficult, particularly since children of this age group are at different reading levels. Even children reading independently should still have adults reading books to them at their interest level, but at a more difficult reading level. Thus, three lists follow—one for those learning to read independently, a second list of good picture books and easy stories to read to children this age, and the third, a small sampling of some recommended informational books. As mentioned previously, it is suggested you consult the bibliography of Resource Books at the end of Chapter 3 of this book for guides for other selections (see Fig. 3 1). You may also wish to consult the list of books, also in Chapter 3, of anthologies suitable for families with several young children of different ages (see Fig. 3.2).

Series Books for Beginning Readers

Berenstain, Stan, and Berenstain, Jan. ''Berenstain Bear'' series.

Christian, Mary Blount. ''Swamp Monsters'' series.

Ehrlich, Amy. ''Leo, Zack and Emmie'' series.

Hoban, Lillian. ''Arthur'' series.

Krensky, Stephen. ''Lionel'' series.

Lobel, Arnold. ''Frog and Toad'' series.

Marshall, James. ''Fox'' series.

Minarik, Else. ''Little Bear'' series.

Parish, Peggy. ''Amelia Bedelia'' series.

Pilkey, Dav. ''Dragon'' series.

Ross, Pat. ''M and M'' series.

Rylant, Cynthia. ''Henry and Mudge'' series.

Seuss, Dr. ''Cat in the Hat'' series.

Sharmat, Marjorie. ''Nate the Great'' series.

Van Leeuwen, Jean. ''Oliver and Amanda'' series.

Wiseman, Bernard. ''Morris and Borris'' series.

Yolen, Jan. ''Commander Toad'' series.

FIGURE 2.1 Continued

Picture Books and Easy Stories

Ahlberg, Janet. *Jolly Postman.* Boston: Little, Brown,1986.

A story about a postman who delivers letters and postcards to storybook characters. Children will know the fairy tale characters and will delight in taking the actual letters, postcards, and invitations out of the envelopes in the book and reading them. This will encourage children's independent writing.

Cleary, Beverly. *Ramona the Pest.* New York: William Morrow & Co., 1968.

One of a series of books about a little girl who gets involved in many humorous escapades at school and with friends. Children six to eight can relate to her assertiveness, argumentativeness, and stubbornness, though she also craves attention and is very competitive.

Fleischman, Sid. *McBroom's Wonderful One-Acre Farm.* New York: Greenwillow, 1992. Also, *Here Comes McBroom!*

Each book contains three tall tales. The silliness of the McBroom adventures should appeal to children this age.

Hurwitz, Johanna. *Russell Sprouts.* Morrow, 1987. Also: *Rip-Roaring Russell; Russell and Elisa;* and *Russell Rides Again.*

The humorous adventures of Russell both at home and at school, the year he enters first grade.

McKissack, Patricia. *Mirandy and Brother Wind.* New York: Knopf, 1988.

Mirandy picks Brother Wind for her partner in the cakewalk contest, but ends up with Ezel, a friend. The story shows Mirandy's competitiveness and desire to be first.

Marshall, James. *Rats on the Roof.* New York: Dial, 1991.

Seven short humorous stories about different animal characters with cartoon illustrations that will appeal to the sense of humor of children at this age.

Milne, A.A. *Winnie-the-Pooh.* New York: Dutton, 1991.

The classic stories of Christopher Robin and his companions, Pooh Bear, Piglet, Eeyore, Kanga, Roo, Rabbit, and Owl. The fantasy of Christopher's toy animals being alive should delight young children.

Scieszka, Jon. *The True Story of the Three Little Pigs.* New York: Viking, 1989. Also, *The Stinky Cheese Man and Other Fairly Stupid Tales.*

Humorous, twisted fairy tales that will delight young listeners who already know the classic tales.

Seeger, Pete. *Abiyoyo.* New York: Macmillan, 1986.

This wonderful tale of a father and son who trick a giant is based on a South African folk story. The story also contains a passage for children to sing along. The elements of magic and the description of the giant will awe young children.

Steig, William. *Sylvester and the Magic Pebble.* Simon & Schuster, 1988.

Sylvester, the donkey, is turned into a rock after finding a magic pebble. Will his family ever see him again? Personified animals and the element of magic lend intrigue.

Thurber, James. *Many Moons.* San Diego: Harcourt Brace, 1943.

A little princess wants the moon and will not be happy until she gets it. Young children will be able to relate to Princess Lenore in this wise, but humorous tale.

FIGURE 2.1 Continued

White, E.B. *Charlotte's Web.* New York: HarperCollins, 1952.

The classic tale of Charlotte the spider who saves the life of Wilbur the pig. Friends and friendship is valued by children of this age.

Informational Books

Arnosky, Jim. *Crinkleroot's Book of Animal Tracking.* New York: Bradbury Press, 1989. Also: *Crinkleroot's Guide to Knowing the Birds; Crinkleroot's Guide to Walking in Wild Places;* and *Crinkleroot's 25 Birds Every Child Should Know.*

These delightful nature and wildlife books have zany, yet informative illustrations and are good for children eager to learn about the outdoors.

Cole, Joanna. *The Magic School Bus Lost in the Solar System.* New York: Scholastic, 1990.

This is one of a series of books—all excellent—that combine a picture book story with facts on various scientific subjects. The comical illustrations and easy-to-read text are a sure hit.

De Regniers, Beatrice Schenk, and others, selectors. *Sing Me a Song of Popcorn.* New York: Scholastic, 1988.

A wonderful selection of both contemporary and older poetry, both serious and humorous, illustrated by nine Caldecott Medal artists. Poems and illustrations will delight all ages.

Heller, Ruth. *Chickens Aren't the Only Ones.* New York: Grosset & Dunlap, 1981. Also: *Plants That Never Ever Bloom;* and *The Reason for a Flower.*

These easy informational books with bright glorious illustrations and facts that read like a story will satisfy children's eagerness to learn.

Kellogg, Steven. *Johnny Appleseed.* New York: Morrow, 1988. Also: *Paul Bunyan;* and *Pecos Bill.*

Kellogg has retold several tall tales and accompanied them with magnificent illustrations sure to appeal to this age group.

Kennedy, X. J., and Kennedy, Dorothy M. *Talking Like the Rain.* Boston: Little, Brown, 1992.

Familiar and contemporary poems are accompanied by bright watercolor paintings. Described as a ''First Book of Poems,'' this will please young poetry listeners.

Nelson, Esther L. *The Funny Song-Book.* New York: Sterling, 1984.

This is just one of several silly song books by this musician. Children will be attracted to the goofy songs and most are old favorites for adults.

Parker, Nancy Winslow, and Joan Richards Wright. *Frogs, Toads, Lizards, and Salamanders.* New York: Greenwillow, 1990.

A companion book is *Bugs.* On the left-hand page is a picture book story, and on the right-hand page a description of the animal mentioned on the left with various parts labeled. This will appeal to those who love nature and the outdoors and will answer questions by young readers eager to learn.

Prelutsky, Jack, selector. *The Random House Book of Poetry.* New York: Random, 1983.

572 mostly funny short poems that will tickle young readers' funny bones.

Schwartz, Alvin. *Ghosts! Ghostly Tales From Folklore.* New York: HarperCollins, 1991. Also, *In a Dark Dark Room and Other Scary Stories.*

Both books are written for those children who have just begun to read independently. Both are also based on familiar folk tales and are just the right amount of ''scary'' for this age group.

FIGURE 2.1 Continued

Simon, Seymour. *Animal Fact/Animal Fable.* New York: Crown, 1979.

    After describing common beliefs about animals and asking if they are fact or fable, answers are provided for each question. Both young children and adults will find this a fun way to learn.

Wallace, Karen. *I Like Monkeys Because* . . . Read and Wonder Books. Cambridge: Candlewick Press, 1993.

    There are several books in this "Read and Wonder" series published by Candlewick Press. All are written and illustrated like a picture book, but contain intriguing facts for those eager to learn.

BIBLIOGRAPHY

Bredekamp, Sue, ed. *Developmentally Appropriate Practice in Early Childhood Programs Serving Children From Birth Through Age 8.* exp. ed. Washington, D.C.: National Association for the Education of Young Children, 1988.

Carlson, Ann D. *Early Childhood Literature Sharing Programs in Libraries.* Hamden: Library Professional Publications, 1985.

Carlson, Ann D. *Preschooler and the Library.* Metuchen, N.J.: Scarecrow, 1991.

Coletta, Anthony J., and Kathleen Coletta. *Year Round Activities for Two-Year-Old Children.* West Nyack: Center for Applied Research in Education, 1986. Also, *Year Round Activities for Three-Year-Old Children* and *Year Round Activities for Four-Year-Old Children.*

Cullinan, Bernice. *Literature and the Child.* New York: Harcourt Brace, 1981.

Cullinan, Bernice. "Literature for Young Children." In *Emerging Literacy: Young Children Learn to Read and Write,* edited by Dorothy S. Strickland and Lesley Mandel Morrow. Newark: International Reading Association, 1989.

Friedes, Harriet. *Preschool Resource Guide.* New York: Plenum Press, 1993.

Herr, Judy, and Yvonne Libby. *Creative Resources for the Early Childhood Classroom.* Albany: Delmar Publishers, 1990.

Hildebrand, Verna. *Guiding Young Children.* 4th ed. New York: Macmillan, 1990.

Huck, Charlotte S., Susan Hepler, and Janet Hickman. *Children's Literature in the Elementary School.* 4th ed. New York: Holt, Rinehart and Winston, 1987.

Jalongo, Mary Renck. *Young Children and Picture Books: Literature From Infancy to Six.* Washington, D.C.: National Association for the Education of Young Children, 1988.

Lamme, Linda L. *Growing Up Reading.* Washington, D.C.: Acropolis Books, 1985.

Lamme, Linda L. *Raising Readers: A Guide to Sharing Literature With Young Children.* New York: Walker and Company, 1980.

McCracken, Janet B. *Off to a Sound Start: Your Baby's First Year.* Washington, D.C.: National Association for the Education of Young Children, 1986.

Miller, Karen. *Ages and Stages.* Owings Mills, Md.: Telshare Publishing, 1985.

Morrison, George S. *Early Childhood Education Today.* 5th ed. New York: Macmillan, 1991.

Morrow, Lesley Mandell. *Literacy Development in the Early Years: Helping Children Read and Write.* Englewood Cliffs: Prentice Hall, 1989.

Norton, Donna E. *Through the Eyes of a Child: An Introduction to Children's Literature.* 2nd ed. Columbus: Merrill, 1987.

Oppenheim, Joanne, Barbara Brenner, and Betty Boegehold. *Choosing Books for Kids.* New York: Ballantine, 1986.

Shaffer, David R. *Developmental Psychology.* Pacific Grove: Brooks/Cole Publishing, 1988.

Sutherland, Zena, and May Hill Arbuthnot. *Children and Books.* Glenview: Scott Foresmen and Company, 1986.

Thomas, James L. *Play, Learn and Grow.* New Providence: Bowker, 1992.

White, Burton L. *The First Three Years of Life.* New York: Prentice Hall, 1990.

3 FAMILY LIBRARY PROGRAMS ON THE IMPORTANCE OF READING TO YOUNG CHILDREN

One of the programs most commonly offered by libraries for caregivers of young children in addition to family storytimes is a workshop, which re-emphasizes the importance of reading to young children. Even though these programs are geared to the caregivers, young children often attend. For the first part of the program, children may be in another area, enjoying stories, an art activity, or literature-based public-performance video. They then join caregivers as the librarian models how to read aloud by sharing stories with the children in attendance. Many libraries have secured grants to help establish such programs.

There are numerous books and articles on this subject that will be helpful when planning such a workshop. The information provided in this chapter will be a simplified version of this material that can be presented in a lecture. Consideration will also be given to family-literacy programs for adults who are at low literacy levels, and find it difficult, embarrassing, or frustrating to read to their young children.

Chapter 2 outlined the developmental characteristics of young children and the implications for sharing books. In addition, types of books and suggested titles for each developmental stage were listed. This information will be useful when presenting this kind of workshop. The titles that are listed are just examples—librarians can pick their own favorites as long as they "fit" the developmental stage. To round out the program, list reasons why it is important to read aloud, and give tips to make reading aloud not only fun but also a family ritual. Ideas for these two sections of your talk follow. Other sample lectures can be found in the American Library Association publication *First Steps to Literacy: Library Programs for Parents, Teachers, and Caregivers.*[1]

THE IMPORTANCE OF READING ALOUD TO YOUNG CHILDREN

There are many books that can serve as good guides on the importance of sharing books with young children—books by Dorothy Butler, Jim Trelease, Linda Lamme, and Mary Margaret Kimmel, to name just a few. A bibliography of these resources follows (see Fig. 3.1). Every librarian should be familiar with these titles and have them on display when presenting such a workshop. However, do not assume most caregivers will want to check these books out—more often, they will rely on titles you actually share enthusiastically during the workshop—so make sure you share a lot of good books! It is a compliment that they depend on your advice, and this can be the start of a good relationship, particularly if they continue to come to the library and ask for your advice selecting books.

Though entire books have been written on the subject of the importance of reading aloud to children, a few points will be reiterated here that you may wish to discuss at the beginning of your talk.

1. The single most important activity for building the knowledge required for eventual success in reading, is reading aloud to children.[2]
2. Literacy development begins at birth, and the early years are crucial for the formation of these skills.
3. Caregivers who read to children contribute directly to their early literacy development.
4. Children's literacy skills often reflect those of their parents.[3]
5. Children who are read to before attending school are more likely to read before reaching school or will learn how to read much easier when taught in school.[4] Learning to read and enjoying reading will help with other subjects in school, because one needs to be able to read to understand any other subject.
6. Children learn to want to read by watching the parent reading for his or her own pleasure. Reading aloud to children is not enough—caregivers must also read by themselves and demonstrate that they enjoy reading.
7. Sharing books can be a very pleasant experience for caregivers and children alike. Each family can have its own special way and time to share books.

FIGURE 3.1 Resource Books on Reading Aloud to Children

Brenner, Barbara, Betty Boegehold, and Joanne Oppenheim. *Choosing Books for Children: How to Choose the Right Book for the Right Child at the Right Time.* New York: Ballantine, 1986.

Butler, Dorothy. *Babies Need Books.* New York: Atheneum, 1982.

Butler, Dorothy, and Marie Clay. *Reading Begins At Home.* Updated ed. Portsmouth, N.H.: Heinemann, 1987.

Cullinan, Bernice E. *Read to Me: Raising Kids Who Love to Read.* New York: Scholastic, 1992.

Cullinan, Bernice E. *Let's Read About-: Finding Books They'll Love to Read.* New York: Scholastic, 1993.

Donavin, Denise Perry, Ed. *Best of the Best for Children.* New York: Random, 1992.

Freeman, Judy. *Books Kids Will Sit Still For: The Complete Read-Aloud Guide.* Rev. ed. New York: Bowker, 1990.

Hearne, Betsy. *Choosing Books for Children.* Rev. ed. New York: Delacorte, 1990.

Jalongo, Mary Renck. *Young Children and Picture Books.* Washington, D.C.: National Association for the Education of Young Children, 1988.

Kimmel, Margaret Mary, and Elizabeth Segal. *For Reading Out Loud!* Rev. ed. New York: Bantam Doubleday Dell, 1991.

Lamme, Linda Leonard. *Growing Up Reading.* Washington, D.C.: Acropolis, 1985.

Lamme, Linda Leonard, et al. *Raising Readers: A Guide to Sharing Literature with Young Children.* New York: Walker, 1980.

Larrick, Nancy. *A Parent's Guide to Children's Reading.* 5th rev. ed. New York: Bantam Doubleday Dell, 1983.

Lipson, Eden Ross. *The New York Times Parent's Guide to the Best Books for Children.* Rev. ed. New York: Random, 1991.

Taylor, Denny, and Dorothy S. Strickland. *Family Storybook Reading.* Portsmouth, N.H.: Heinemann, 1986.

Trelease, Jim. *The New Read-Aloud Handbook.* 2nd rev. ed. New York: Penguin, 1989.

8. Reading aloud to children is so important that it should become a daily ritual and is not as effective if only done occasionally.[5]

9. Sharing books with young children cultivates their language and listening skills.

10. It is important to keep reading to young children *even after they have learned to read.* Children have *more* desire to read independently if they are read to. The love of books and sharing stories increases.

11. A love of reading and books does not occur automatically. It is developed by sharing many books with children from a young age, and by making this time spent together an enjoyable experience.

TIPS ON SHARING BOOKS WITH YOUNG CHILDREN

After explaining the importance of reading aloud to young children and allowing time for discussion with the participants, you then may wish to convey some hints on how to share books with young children. Again, for more ideas, you may consult some of the resource books cited above. However, several important tips will be mentioned here:

1. Make sure that reading is a fun time for your child. If the child does not want to listen and the experience becomes frustrating, stop and try again at another time. A baby may not wish to look at a cloth or board book until a couple of months old, but be sure to share language, rhymes, and songs with the infant from birth, and books as soon as possible. Also, an active toddler may not sit still for long. Try for a quiet time before a nap or at bedtime.

2. Read to your child for the pure enjoyment of the story and art. Do not ask the child to point at the words while you are reading. The purpose is not to teach your child to read, but to read for pleasure, so that books and reading will be fun. Do not ask questions to see if your child memorized the text, but it's okay to talk about the story after reading it, and if you ask a question, ask something that will allow the child some creative thought. For example, "What do you think would have happened if . . . ?"

3. Though it is good to go to the public library on a regular basis, also try to purchase some books for your child. For families with small incomes, books can be obtained at used bookstores, thrift shops, garage or yard sales, and public-library book sales. Give books as gifts for birthdays or holidays. Relatives or friends who give gifts to

your child should be encouraged to give books. Give a list of your child's favorite titles ahead of time if possible to help guide choices.

4. Read aloud everything possible around your home or when out with your child. This includes newspaper stories, magazines, signs or billboards, cereal boxes, recipes, print on a TV screen, and the like.

5. Have your child draw a picture of the story after reading a book. Ask to the child to dictate a story to you or dictate a message in a letter to a friend or relative.

6. Take a book with you when you leave the house in case you must wait somewhere and have a few spare moments to read.

7. Have older children, babysitters, grandparents, and others read to your child whenever possible. Older children will feel more grown up if asked to read to younger children. If you have several children, let them read to each other or make up stories to go with the pictures in the book.

8. Act out stories with your child. Have your child make up stories or help you make up a story.

9. Make simple puppets and props with your child and use them to tell a story. Encourage your child to tell stories with puppets and props.

10. Sing songs and use rhymes, poems, and chants whenever possible.

11. Involve children in the storytelling whenever possible. Let them finish a rhyme in the book or supply a rhyming word or join in on a repetitive phrase or familiar passage. Have them retell familiar stories or make up a story to go with a wordless book.

12. Read stories with enthusiasm and expression. Change the tone of your voice and adjust the pace of your reading to fit the narration. Use your voice to make the story come alive!

13. Children will often ask for favorite stories to be read again and again. This may seem annoying, but it really does have some positive effects. Soon the child will tell the story with you and may even begin to read some words. Choosing books that you and your child enjoy will create enthusiasm.

14. Do not change words that seem difficult for your child. Explain the word after you read it. This is the way children learn language.

15. Make sure the child can see the pictures and the text that

you are reading. Very young children should sit on your lap, and when older, they should sit next to you. Talk about the pictures in the book after reading the story. Also, at different times during the day, talk about books you have read.

16. Turn off the TV when reading. Make sure family reading time is as important as family TV or video viewing. Children will follow models of adult behavior in the amount of TV/video viewing. If you watch a lot of TV and videos, so will your child.

17. Teach your child how to take care of books. Have special places to store books where the child can reach them. Though there can be several places in the house (bedroom, bathroom, kitchen), make sure they are returned there every day so that the child can reach for them and look at them whenever desired.

18. If children are fidgety, have them scribble, draw, or hold a favorite toy while you are reading.

19. Never use book reading as a punishment for a child, or the child will relate reading books to a negative experience.

20. Try to read aloud every day. Find a special time and stick to it. Just as your child eats and washes every day, try to make reading aloud a habit you do every day also. Children will look forward to this time—knowing it is their own special time to spend with you.

SHOWING BY EXAMPLE/ MODELING READING ALOUD TO CAREGIVERS

After covering the importance of reading aloud to young children from infancy and suggesting tips to make the experience both productive and enjoyable, you will then want to speak directly to caregivers about developmental characteristics of young children and ways to share books that directly relate to the age/stage of the children present. For example, if you are speaking to teen parents of newborns, you would only need to cover the characteristics and implications for book sharing given in Chapter 2 of this book under infants. Remember to gear the information to the audience present. Do not present all the information given if it is too much to absorb, cover only the important points. After sharing information according to the various stages represented in the audience, you will want to spend the majority of your speech time covering books suitable for those ages/stages. It is important that you read numerous books and model ways to share these books. Show caregivers how to encourage children's participation when reading stories. For example, if you are reading *Is Your Mama a Llama?* by Deborah Guarino, you would model for the caregivers how they should pause and allow their children time to supply the answer to the rhyming riddle. By modeling these activities, you will give caregivers ideas of creative ways to share literature. This is probably one of the most important parts of your program. You may also wish to share some anthologies with many different stories contained in one book that would be good for home purchase. These collections are good for families that have children of varying ages. Suggested anthologies follow.

FIGURE 3.2 Sample Anthologies

Big Bear Treasury. Volume One. Cambridge, Mass.: Candlewick Press, 1992. Also, Volume Two.

Brooke, L. Leslie. *The Golden Goose Book.* New York: Clarion, 1992.

Chorao, Kay. *The Baby's Story Book.* New York: Dutton, 1985.

Cole, Joanna. *Read Aloud Treasury.* New York: Doubleday, 1988.

Ehrlich, Amy. *The Random House Book of Fairy Tales.* New York: Random House, 1985.

Impey, Rose. *Read Me a Fairy Tale: A Child's Book of Classic Fairy Tales.* New York: Scholastic, 1993.

Low, Alice. *The Family Read-Aloud Holiday Treasury.* Boston: Little, Brown, 1991. Also, *The Family Read-Aloud Christmas Treasury.*

Mayer, Marianna. *My First Book of Nursery Tales.* New York: Random House, 1983.

Milne, A.A. *Pooh's Bedtime Book.* New York: Dutton, 1980.

Pooley, Sarah. *It's Raining, It's Pouring: A Book for Rainy Days.* New York: Greenwillow, 1993.

Retan, Walter, comp. *Piggies, Piggies, Piggies: A Treasury of Stories, Songs and Poems.* New York: Simon & Schuster, 1993.

Rockwell, Anne. *Three Bears and Fifteen Other Stories.* New York: HarperCollins, 1975.

To Ride A Butterfly: New Pictures, Stories, Folktales, Fables, Nonfiction, Poems, and Songs for Young Children. New York: Bantam Doubleday Dell, 1991.

Seuss, Dr. *Six by Seuss: A Treasury of Dr. Seuss Classics.* New York: Random House, 1991.

Trelease, Jim, ed. *Hey! Listen to This: Stories to Read Aloud.* New York: Penguin, 1992.

Voake, Charlotte. *The Three Little Pigs and Other Favorite Nursery Stories.* Cambridge, Mass.: Candlewick Press, 1991.

Windham, Sophie. *Read Me A Story: A Child's Book of Favorite Tales.* New York: Scholastic, 1991.

WHO IS YOUR AUDIENCE FOR THIS TYPE OF PROGRAM?

Unfortunately, the hard part of conducting this type of workshop is reaching the people that most need to hear your message. Often such workshops will attract caregivers who know the importance of reading aloud but want more ideas of what to read and how to read to their children. Certainly this can be a beneficial program for these caregivers, but reaching those who are unaware of the necessity of reading to a child from birth, or of reading aloud on a daily basis, is even more worthwhile. For this reason, outreach is almost always necessary. Though the program may still be held in the library, it may be necessary to first meet caregivers on their own "turf." Contact social-service agencies, teen parents in schools, day-care providers, or preschool or Head Start centers in the community. After a partnership is established, it may be easier to encourage caregivers to come to the library for such a workshop. Many libraries succeed by holding two separate programs—one out in an agency first, and then a follow-up program in the library so caregivers can receive library cards and check out books. More about outreach will be discussed in Chapter 7.

LOW-INCOME FAMILIES

Do not assume that families of lower socioeconomic levels are not literate or have no contact with books. Taylor and Dorsey-Gaines, in their classic publication *Growing Up Literate,* did a study of an urban, poverty-stricken area where families were African-American and mostly single-parent. Though the families they studied were living in poverty, many of the children grew up literate and families used their literacy for a wide assortment of purposes, though it did not free them from poverty. They discovered that sex, race, economic status, and setting could not be used as significant correlates of literacy. The myths and stereotypes that create the image of poor families, inner-city families, and families led by teenage mothers as not being literate had no relevance.[6] They did find however, that education and literacy cannot be used interchangeably. Some of the people they interviewed were highly literate, but not educated in the traditional sense of the word. Most of the people's reading was of environmental print. Thus the researchers found that it was the literacy environment that was important, and that this environment could be found in homes differing in occupations and socioeconomic levels. William Teale also did a study of low-income families (Anglo, African-American, and Mexican-American) in San Diego, and found vast differences in the literacy experiences among the families, including a great difference in the number of literacy activities, the degree of parental involvement, and the amount of time children spent reading and writing. The amount of reading and writing materials in the home varied, along with the degree of parental interaction.[7] His conclusions also confirmed that economic factors or ethnicity did not account for the differences he found. Dolores Durkin conducted an investigation of poor African-American children who were successful readers and found some preschool children read prior to coming to school. In analyzing those families, Durkin found encouraging adults who gave a lot of attention to their child, and also older children in the household who enjoyed playing school with the preschool children, often reading to them. The families showed an interest in school and the child's success in it.[8] Spiegel, Fitzgerald, and Cunningham's research found that parents have different perceptions of what is effective for their young child's literacy development. Highly literate parents and less literate parents differed in several opinions. For example, low-literacy parents tended to put more importance on skill-based or instruction-oriented activities than high-literacy parents.[9] Another researcher found that many low-income families do not know how to contribute to a learning environment. For many in Mavrogenes' study, family maintenance or survival was a key concern. Few energies were left to spend on educational pursuits.[10] These parents need to be convinced that no matter how stressful life is, that a few minutes daily spent reading a book, sharing stories or songs, and listening and talking to their children alleviates stress and even helps children feel more peaceful and safe.

Patricia Edwards videotaped parents of lower socioeconomic status reading to their children and found that many did not ask questions or carry on any type of conversation with their child. They were also more apt to punish their children if they did not listen. Many had difficulty with their own reading skills. Her message is that we need not only to emphasize to parents the benefits of reading to their children, but we need to show them how to do it.[11] This should be the role of the librarian when presenting this type of workshop. Most caregivers will not need to be convinced of the importance of reading to their children, as much as they need to learn how to do it and what good books are available to share. Dr. Edwards completed a literacy training program called *Parents as Partners in Reading.* Three videos accompany a training manual, which is to be used by facilitators to train parents of kindergarten through third grade children to read effectively to their children. Videos emphasize the following topics: the importance of reading to children, creating a positive reading environment, modeling reading behavior, and roles parents play in shared reading.[12]

OTHER SAMPLE PROGRAMS

Some libraries will hold a series of parent programs, with the above lecture as one of the sessions. During other weeks, community-resource people talk about such subjects as children's health and nutrition; child development; parenting; the importance of play; educational and safe toys; child safety; and discipline. Usually these programs are held in the evening and a different program is held each week. Children of parent participants are often in another room enjoying a storytime or art activities.

Libraries have had success with other types of parenting workshops that not only encourage reading aloud to children, but also cover other developmentally appropriate activities for the child's emergent literacy skills. Two such programs are profiled here (see Fig. 3.3).

FAMILY-LITERACY PROGRAMS

Family-literacy programs are aimed at families where the caregiver has a low literacy level or is illiterate. It has been proven that modeling reading to young children by the caregiver is crucial and that the primary caregiver plays a major role in the young child's emergent literacy skills. Thus, children at risk for low literacy levels reside with caregivers who have low literacy levels. Not only do the children miss having good role models, but they are not helped with school and homework problems in the same way as children with more literate caregivers. The only way to prevent this low literacy cycle from repeating itself is by helping caregivers improve their literacy levels while their children are still young. Many pub-

FIGURE 3.3 Parent/Child Workshop

Contact Person: Sandra Feinberg

Library: Middle Country Public Library, Centereach, N.Y.

Brief Description: This workshop is for parents or caregivers of children ages one through three. Programs are held five consecutive weeks for one hour and 15 minutes at a time. The large room where the workshops are held is 30 by 41 feet; also held in rooms 22 by 30 feet. Arranged in this area are books, puzzles, blocks, infant toys, arts and crafts, an alpine house gym, a tunnel, puppets and dolls, gross motor equipment, trucks and cars, musical instruments, a housekeeping and dress-up area, and a resource area. Approximately 22 families attend at one time and sessions are held in the early morning and mid-morning. The librarian makes sure that families are comfortable and have the ability to move around from one station to another. A resource professional is available every week to speak on such topics as: speech and language; child development; play; and nutrition. The resource person speaks to small groups or individually on a one-to-one basis. A paraprofessional with early childhood education background handles the art activities area. The success of the program has been overwhelming and several community coalitions have formed as a result of the workshop. Over 21 Suffolk County Libraries and 10 New York State libraries now conduct the program.

Source: Feinberg, Sandra. "The Parent/Child Workshop: A Unique Program." *School Library Journal,* April 1985. Also, *Running A Parent/Child Workshop: A How-To-Do-It Manual for Librarians.* Neal-Schuman Publishers, 1995.

Parent-Child Learning Centers

Contact Person: Pat Rogers

Library: Johnson County Library System, Shawnee Mission, Kansas

Brief Description: The Parent-Child Learning Centers began as an alternative approach to library programming for preschoolers. The centers are placed in an area of the children's library. Parents and children have a chance to interact together with hands-on games, open-ended art activities, music, and physical activities. The objective is to enhance the development of prereading skills and involve the parent in the child's learning process. Most activities are geared toward language development and preliteracy skills. Signs are included with each activity with suggestions for interaction. Handouts are provided explaining curriculum themes and concepts, suggestions for reinforcing activities at home, and a list of appropriate books. The librarian often serves as a model, showing the parent how to involve a child in an activity or to introduce books. Unlike story programs, learning centers allow one-on-one interaction with the caregiver; flexible time schedules since caregivers can drop in at any time; no sign-up; no age limit; and no group size limits. Several different curricula rotate among branches in the library system.

Source: Rogers, Pat, and Barbara Herrin. "Parent-Child Learning Centers: An Alternative Approach to Library Programming for Preschoolers." *Top of the News,* Summer 1986.

lic libraries play an important role in helping them reach this goal. However, it requires a great deal of cooperation among departments of a library, community agencies, and local organizations involved with adult literacy. Outreach for this type of program is essential—you can feel certain that most low-literacy caregivers are not using their public library.

Family-literacy programs in libraries can accomplish several goals in addition to the modeling mentioned above: increase the literacy skills of both caregivers and children; cultivate a positive attitude toward both reading and writing (for example, family biographies can be written or dictated); and encourage families to practice literacy activities on a daily basis.

For librarians who serve youth, this is one program you should not attempt alone. Many libraries form partnerships with vocational schools, community colleges, and local literacy organizations such as Literacy Volunteers of America. It takes much teamwork to coordinate this, but few programs can be more rewarding. There is real satisfaction in seeing the joy of caregivers when they can successfully share books with their young children in a way that brings great pleasure to them, as well as increases their self-esteem.

The first step is to find out what local literacy agencies are in your area. You do not want to duplicate what they are already doing, but rather work with them toward a common goal. However, you need to be careful when forming such a partnership. Their objectives may be quite different from yours. Make sure you both have the same goals and objectives and that you are in agreement on the type of program you plan to offer.

Next, target a certain group you want to serve. It could be teen parents or low-literacy caregivers. Heads of social-service agencies may be able to help you target an audience. This is where your second partnership is formed—with agencies in the community that have contact with those you wish to serve. Advertise, but do not expect to distribute flyers that must be read. You may hang some posters (written in the simplest language possible and with graphics) and advertise at grocery stores, welfare sites, food-stamp or unemployment offices, health-care offices, laundromats, churches, or public-transportation stops in the area. Other forms of media, such as radio and television, cable ads, videotapes, or billboards may also be beneficial.

After establishing your initial goals and objectives, you will then need to go to where your target audience is. Have your first meeting with your target audience in a location familiar to them. Talk to them and tailor your program to their needs. One or two initial programs can be done at this location. You can describe what the library has to offer. Once you have won their confidence, it will be easier to establish a program in the library. For example, you may wish to contact the Parent Coordinator at your local Head Start site and have that person help identify a target audience. With the Parent Coordinator's help, you can attend some Head Start Parent Meetings and present a story program for the parents and children together. Then try to have your next meeting or program at the library, showing what resources you have.

There are many obstacles to overcome when trying to attract low-literacy or illiterate caregivers to a family-literacy program. Jeffrey and Charles Salter mention several in their book *Literacy and the Library*:

1. *False Pride:* People are too proud to accept help.
2. *Fear of Exposure:* There is a stigma attached to not knowing how to read and write, and many people want to keep their inabilities confidential.
3. *Fear of Program Equipment:* Modern equipment used by literacy trainers, such as books on tape and computers, may intimidate people.
4. *Fear of Personal Treatment in the Program:* There can be feelings of failure or of being looked down on.
5. Some materials may seem childish and inappropriate to an adult.
6. *Transportation to the Family Literacy Program:* Lack of a car, public transportation, or money to use public transportation are difficult problems to overcome. Free bus passes may be an answer.[13]

If you have literacy tutors in your library, and the tutors are meeting with caregivers separately while you are doing a program for the children by themselves, arrange to have some time when the caregivers are in the room with the children. Caregivers need to learn more than just how to read more successfully—they need to see you model story and language experiences. When the children are animated and listening to your stories, rhymes, songs, and finger plays, the caregivers will be encouraged to share such experiences with their children. Another important component is to allow time for the caregivers to practice their learned skills by sharing books with their children in the library setting.

If you have any way to distribute free books, this is an excellent idea. These books will be treasured. Even if you convince caregivers to get library cards and check out books for their children, there is nothing more important than children owning books of their own. You may also wish to give out certificates of attendance or other motivational rewards.

Do not feel that your program is a failure if people do not come back to the library or do not check out books. You may reach only a few people in each program, but you can never really measure what effect your program might have on a family in the future.

Even the most basic programs will require some special funding. Some funds may be covered by your library's annual budget and other cooperating agencies may contribute some capital. There is also some federal funding in support of family literacy. In addition to Library Services and Construction Act monies (Titles I & VI), there are also funds available through the Elementary and Secondary Education Act. To receive more information on these types of funding, check the Clearinghouse on Adult Education and Literacy under the U.S. Department of Education, Washington, D.C.

There have been three strong initiatives in the United States to fund family-literacy programs. They include the Bell Atlantic/American Library Association Family Literacy Project, California's Families for Literacy (FFL) program, and the Cargill/American Library Association Partnership for Family Literacy Programs. They are described briefly here, though much more information can be found in *Library-Based Family Literacy Projects* by Margaret Monsour and Carole Talan.[14]

The Bell Atlantic/ALA Family Literacy Project was established in 1989. The Office of Library Outreach Services, part of the American Library Association, administers this project and funding comes from the Bell Atlantic Foundation. Over one million dollars have been distributed thus far and funding continues, as of this writing, through December 1994. This is a regional project and libraries in the states of Virginia, West Virginia, New Jersey, Delaware, Pennsylvania, Maryland, and the District of Columbia may apply. The goal of the project is "to encourage solutions to the problem of low literacy by developing local partnerships in communities among libraries, adult basic-education specialists and literacy providers, and a local business partner, and through the implementation of library-based family-literacy programs."[15]

The California State Library established a state-wide program called Families for Literacy in 1988. Funding is provided to local libraries to expand their adult-literacy services to include families with adult learners who have a preschool child. Some of the provisions required to receive funding include providing books for ownership; holding meetings in libraries and introducing the families to the resources and services available; providing storytelling, word games, and other enjoyable reading-oriented activities for families; encouraging the use of children's books for tutoring and language-experience stories from the family programs as adult-literacy instructional materials; teaching parents how to select books and read aloud to children; providing services that enhance family participation and foster a family environment for reading; and helping parents gain access to books on parenting, child care, health, nutrition, and education.[16]

The Cargill/American Library Association Partnership for Family Literacy has granted numerous $1,000 awards to local libraries or literacy agencies each year since 1992. The project encourages the development of partnerships in the community between Cargill Grain locations, public libraries, literacy providers, and other community organizations. Cargill hopes that the projects will serve as models for replication in other communities in the U.S. Over 150 project partnerships in 26 states and 20 countries have been developed as of 1993.[17] Programs have been developed in both small towns and large urban areas. In addition to libraries, Cargill has teamed up with "4H, Scouts, literacy councils, community colleges, adult basic-education programs, homeless shelters, booster clubs, Head Start, food shelves, and preschools."[18]

There are several resources you can consult to read more about examples of family-literacy programs. A bibliography at the end of this chapter lists several sources (see Fig. 3.5). A few programs will be highlighted here as samples, though others will be cited in Chapter 7 of this book (see Fig. 3.4).

ENDNOTES

1. Preschool Services and Parent Education Committee, Association for Library Service to Children, *First Steps to Literacy: Library Programs for Parents, Teachers, and Caregivers.* (Chicago: American Library Association, 1990).
2. M. Binkley, *Becoming a Nation Of Readers: What Parents Can Do.* (Washington, D.C.: Office of Educational Research and Improvement, 1988).
3. P. Weinberg, *Family Literacy and the School.* (Syracuse: New Reader's Press, 1990).
4. Denny Taylor and Dorothy S. Strickland, *Family Storybook Reading.* (Portsmouth, N.H.: Heinemann, 1986), p. 15.
5. Timothy Rasinski and A. D. Fredericks, "Sharing Literacy: Guiding Principles and Practices for Parent Involvement," *Reading Teacher,* Vol. 41, Issue 6, 1988.

FIGURE 3.4 Success by Six

Contact Person: Ginger Bush and Kathleen Johnson

Library: Minneapolis Public Library, Minneapolis, Minn.

Brief Description: A partnership was established between the Minneapolis Health Department and the Library, with a special project manager for the program. It united the strengths of both library and health professionals in reaching out to families/parents with low literacy levels. Funding was by the United Way of Minneapolis. Developmentally appropriate books and toys were introduced to parents with children under the age of two years. Books and toys were selected jointly by library staff and health professionals, with the goal of picking materials that would support literacy through the normal sensorimotor experiences of young children. Items picked included various board books, oversized crayons and paper, blocks in a container, balls, and safety mirrors. The *Five Owls* journal staff helped produce a "Yes You Can!" poster that focused on the developmental milestones of early childhood and depicted caregivers introducing babies to books. The books, toys, and posters were packaged for distribution at six different children's health clinics in the city. Nurses were trained by library staff to use materials with families during clinic visits. Families also received book lists, library card applications and a map with library locations and were encouraged to use the library.

Source: Bush, Ginger. "Let's Start at the Beginning." *Five Owls,* March/April 1992: 86-87.

Start Smart

Library: Seattle Public Library, Seattle, Wash.

Brief Description: "Start Smart: A Family Learning Program" is sponsored by the Seattle Public Library and is funded by the Boeing Company, a memorial fund and two foundations. Goals are to help parents and children enjoy reading and writing, have fun learning together, and learn about the library. This free family learning program is designed for caregivers who want to improve their reading and also to help their three- to ten-year-old children succeed in school. Several community agencies work with the library including the Literacy Action Center, the Goodwill Literacy Adult Learning Center, the Seattle Education Center, The Southwest Seattle Literacy Coalition, Mt. Zion Ethnic School, and the Southeast Family Support Center. Families listen to stories told by a librarian, get library cards, check out books, and make family books. Individually caregivers meet to discuss ways to help their children learn. They also practice reading children's books together while the children hear stories, make puppets, paint, and write. Start Smart programs meet once a week in different locations around Seattle. Volunteers help staff the programs.

Source: Seattle Public Library Brochure.

FIGURE 3.5 Family Literacy Programming Bibliography

California State Library Foundation. *Families for Literacy.* Produced by the California State Library. 15 min. Sacramento: California State Library Foundation, 1992. Videocassette and guidebook.

First Teachers: A Family Literacy Handbook for Parents, Policy-Makers, and Literacy Providers. Washington, D.C.: Barbara Bush Foundation for Family Literacy, 1989.

McIvor, M. Conlon, ed. *Family Literacy in Action: A Survey of Successful Programs.* Syracuse: New Readers Press, 1990.

Monsour, Margaret, and Carole Talan. *Library-Based Family Literacy Projects.* Chicago: American Library Association, 1993.

Preschool Services and Parent Education Committee. *First Steps to Literacy: Library Programs for Parents, Teachers, and Caregivers.* Chicago: American Library Association, 1990.

Salter, Jeffrey L., and Charles A. Salter. *Literacy and the Library.* Englewood, Colo.: Libraries Unlimited, 1991.

---

6. Denny Taylor and Catherine Dorsey-Gaines, *Growing Up Literate.* (Portsmouth, N.H.: Heinemann, 1986), p. 201.
7. William Teale, "Emergent Literacy as a Perspective for Examining how Young Children Became Writers and Readers," in *Emergent Literacy: Writing and Reading,* eds. W. Teale and E. Sulzby. (Norwood, N.J.: Ablex, 1986).
8. Delores Durkin, "Poor Black Children Who Are Successful Readers," *Urban Education,* Vol. 19, Issue 1, 1984.
9. Dixie Lee Spiegel, Jill Fitzgerald, and James W. Cunningham, "Parental Perceptions of Preschoolers' Literacy Development: Implications for Home-School Partnerships," *Young Children,* Vol. 48, No. 5, 1993.
10. N. Mavrogenes, "Helping Parents Help Their Children Become Literate," *Young Children,* Vol. 45, No. 5, 1990.
11. Patricia Edwards, "Supporting Lower SES Mothers' Attempts To Provide Scaffolding for Book Reading, " in *Risk Makers Risk Takers Risk Breakers: Reducing the Risks for Young Literacy Learners,* eds. J.B. Allen and J. M Mason. (Portsmouth, N.H.: Heinemann, 1989).
12. Patricia Edwards, *Parents as Partners in Reading: A Family Literacy Training Program.* (Chicago: Children's Press, 1990).
13. Jeffrey L. Salter and Charles A. Salter, *Literacy and the Library.* (Englewood, Colo.: Libraries Unlimited, 1991), pp. 84-89.
14. Margaret Monsour and Carole Talan, *Library-Based Family Literacy Projects.* (Chicago: American Library Association, 1993).
15. Ibid., p. v.

16. Ibid., pp. xvi-xvii.

17. Information from a Cargill Grain pamphlet distributed at the Preconference sponsored by the Office for Library Outreach Services of the American Library Association held June 24-25, 1993, in New Orleans, La., entitled "Family Literacy: What It Is, What Librarians Can Do."

18. Ibid.

4 FAMILY STORYTIME PROGRAMS, INCLUDING INFANT PROGRAMS, TODDLER PROGRAMS, AND PRESCHOOL PROGRAMS

HISTORY OF STORY PROGRAMS IN PUBLIC LIBRARIES

Probably the most common program for young children in public libraries today is the preschool storytime. As Ann Carlson noted in her excellent resource *The Preschooler and the Library,* these programs, typically for children ages three through five, started in the 1930s. Children's librarians that began this type of program did so as a way to "broaden their library service" by expanding what was typically provided at that time, storytimes for children ages six to 15.[1] With the introduction of children's rooms, an increase in the number of picture books being produced, and an interest in early childhood education, the idea quickly caught on, even for librarians reluctant to start such programs. As Carlson notes, many parents began to ask for such programs for their young children and would bring their preschoolers to storytimes for school-age children, much to the dismay of librarians. Some parents not only initiated the programs, but also conducted them.[2] By the 1940s, an increasing number of articles about preschool storytimes appeared and textbooks used in training children's librarians contained information on executing this type of program.[3] By the 1950s, these storytimes were becoming a regular part of library service in public libraries, but with the majority of libraries not inviting parents into the storytime area.[4] Many librarians, even today, feel that this should be the child's first independent experience without the caregiver, and the young child's first group experience. But with today's changing society, many children have their first group experience long before the age of four or five. In a study by the U.S. Department of Education, during the spring of 1991, parents of about 80 percent of preschool children reported that their children were either currently being cared for by someone other than themselves, or were attending an early education program on a regular basis, or had received such care or education.[5] So for many children, too much time is spent apart from the caregiver, and storytimes instead can become one of the few times in the caregiver's and child's busy life when time can be spent together. A caregiver present in preschool storytime programs is vital due to the modeling done by the librarian. With this experience, caregivers are better equipped to share books, rhymes, and songs with their young children and are more apt to do so.

Toddler programs are much more common in libraries today than infant programming, which is still on the rise. The success of *Mother Goose Time,* a book written on infant programming by Jane Marino and Dorothy Houlihan (H.W. Wilson), has given more librarians the practical help and confidence they need in programming for the very young and their caregivers. It is hard to ascertain exactly when infant and toddler programming began in libraries, but the Association for Library Service to Children sponsored a preconference at the American Library Association Conference in San Francisco in 1987 where several librarians spoke of lapsit programs they had successfully held since the 1970s. *School Library Journal* records the San Francisco Public Library's outstanding series of programs entitled "You, Your New Baby and the Library,"[6] which were held in 1978. Though toddler programs will probably be more common than infant programs in libraries, both are vital, particularly if one remembers the importance of reading to children from infancy. Many libraries have distributed booklets such as "Catch Them in the Cradle" to new caregivers in hospitals, or have given coupons to parents of newborns to bring to the library to exchange for a free book.

GENERAL GUIDELINES FOR STORY PROGRAMS

Storytimes for young children and their caregivers introduce them to what the library has to offer. Thus it is ideal to hold these programs in the library, where caregivers and children can check out books and other materials. However, some of the people you most need to reach may not come to the library or know about library programs, no matter how they are publicized. Because these are often the people that would benefit the most, it is highly recommended that you consider doing some outreach story programs. More will be discussed on outreach in Chapters 7 and 8 of this book. Approach social agencies in your community that have contact with young children, such as Well Baby Clinics; child-care programs in vocational schools; Head Start programs that incorporate parental-involvement programs; family-caregiver associations; and day-care centers.

Programs held for young children and their caregivers in the library normally require preregistration. However, when doing programs outside of the library, this will probably not be possible. A librarian must be more adaptable, having books with short texts, and active rhymes and songs. The length of the program, or the activities used, may need to be adjusted in midstream. Planning more than what you need is advantageous—then deciding what is most appropriate while you are executing the program—will allow more flexibility.

Storytimes held for children younger than age three are really not programs for the children, but are meant for the caregiver, because children at this age are really not developmentally ready for a group storytime experience. However, these experiences are very important, so that the caregiver knows how to share literature with the young child from infancy. Many caregivers are uncertain how to read to their children using expression and how to extend the language experience, which the librarian can model. Requiring caregiver participation means librarians can urge them to read, talk, and sing to their infant or toddler at home. Often, caregivers reading to their infant will get frustrated, feeling that the baby is not really listening. Librarians can encourage the caregiver to keep reading time short and to stop if the baby is crying and not enjoying the experience. They can also explain that it is customary for babies to try to hit the pages, grab the book, or chew on the book—this is normal development, and caregivers need to persevere and learn how to adjust to their infants' responses. Telling the caregivers what to expect and how to handle different situations that arise will make for a better program for all involved.

Programs for children under the age of three are not just shorter versions of preschool storytimes. Rather, they consist of sharing board and cloth books, or very simple picture books, rhymes, and songs developmentally appropriate for infants and toddlers. For librarians still reluctant to engage in programming for caregivers of infants and toddlers, it is important to remember that literacy begins at birth, and by ignoring children at this level of development in programming, the library is avoiding serving the youngest of children. Libraries are in the business to serve community members through the entire life span.

STORY PROGRAMS FOR INFANTS AND CAREGIVERS

Story programs for infants (newborns through 12 to 18 months) are really programs for the caregiver of the infant—the baby attends so the adult can practice! Very few infants will intently watch the action performed by the librarian. However, by having the infant along, caregivers can practice rhymes and songs with their child. The librarian's purpose is three-fold: to build onto what the parent already knows; to model sharing books, rhymes, and songs with newborns; and to encourage caregivers to continue these activities at home.

Some librarians question the value of infant/caregiver programs. Yet infants are another part of the public that public libraries should be serving. There are numerous benefits to conducting infant/caregiver programs. Probably the most significant is that few people, even those knowledgeable on topics such as literacy, are aware of the importance of reading, talking, and singing to the newborn from birth. Particularly, many feel they should start reading to a child at age one or two, or when they feel the child will listen and respond. Also, some caregivers do not know how to share board or cloth books with newborns. Many of these books contain few, if any, words. Adults may be unaware of how to extend the texts by adding their own words, leading to a rewarding language and listening experience for their infant. Even infants can begin to learn what books are and that they are important. The child, exposed to language, develops observation and listening skills. Newborns also respond to music and rhyme. They enjoy being touched and held by the caregiver and receive needed attention.

An infant/caregiver program is not a "watered-down" toddler or preschool program. Books, music, and rhymes shared must be suitable for newborns. Unlike most libraries' preschool and toddler programs, infant storytimes are not thematically arranged. Babies are not aware of a theme and it is more crucial to share developmentally appropriate activities with caregivers so that they can, in return, practice the activities at home. It is also not necessary to have a series of programs. If staffing permits a series, this is ideal, but more crucial is reaching those caregivers who do not realize the significance of reading, talking, and singing to their child from infancy. One or two programs are fine. You can have one program a week for two or three weeks, or one program a month, or even one program in the spring and one in the fall. Again, it is more vital to reach those who need this type of program the most, rather than those who already know the importance of reading to their child from infancy. The number of potential people to reach can be very large. Having fewer programs and reaching more people is preferable. Using the time to train others who have contact with infants and their caregivers will permit more people to be reached.

Ideally, the programs should be in the early evening hours so that working parents can attend. A Saturday program is another good choice. However, if both of these are impossible, make sure your programs are in the morning and not during baby nap times. If the program is being held in the library, it is a good idea to have participants preregister, so you will know what size group to expect. If you are doing outreach with a community organization or agency, you may not know the number of participants ahead of time and will need to be more flexible. The program should be limited to ten to 15 caregivers with their infants. If you need to have more at one time, keep the group sharing time short. It would be better to have two smaller sessions back-to-back instead of one large group. If you do hold two sessions back-to-back, make sure you have enough resource books. Duplicate copies of excellent resources are fine—just make sure you have enough copies for adults to check out and take home.

Many times you will find older children attending with the infant, because it is not always possible for caregivers to attend such activities without bringing older children along. It is ideal to have the infant and caregiver alone, but this is another area where one must adapt. Caregivers should also be discouraged from bringing more than one infant. Because the caregiver will be working with the infant, it is next to impossible to deal with two infants at the same time. However, one would not want to deter a caregiver of twins from attending, so a hard and fast rule on this is not possible.

For the program, adults sit in a circle on the floor or on a rug or mats. This way, everyone is a part of the group and can see the librarian, who also sits in the circle. Sitting on the floor also permits the librarian to be at the baby's eye level.

The program should be divided into two parts. One part is a group sharing time of approximately 20 minutes. During this time, simple rhymes and songs are shared so that the adult can sing, touch, lift, and jostle the baby. First, have the caregivers introduce themselves and their babies. Then proceed with the program. The sample programs that follow consist of: 1. an opening song; 2. the sharing of a book; 3. four rhymes, each of which should be repeated twice, and consisting of one finger/hand rhyme, one toe/foot rhyme, one tickle/touch rhyme, and one bounce/lift rhyme; 4. sharing a cloth book; 5. sharing a board book; 6. four more rhymes, each repeated twice, and as above, one finger/hand rhyme, one toe/foot rhyme, one tickle/touch rhyme, and one bounce/lift rhyme; 7. a song or lullaby; and 8. a closing song. Books shared should be board and cloth books, with the librarian modeling how to expand the one- or two-word texts with language. When reading the books, demonstrate how you point-and-name the object, then extend the text. For example, "Here's a cow. The cow goes 'Moo-Moo.'" A list of the activities and the order you wish to do them in should be kept near you so that you can quickly move from one activity to the next. It helps to have a teddy bear or suitable doll to demonstrate the lap rhymes. A take-home sheet with rhymes and songs that you used plus additional ones good for infant sharing should be provided, especially if you are having only one or two sessions. This encourages caregivers to continue the experience at home. The caregiver is then equipped with rhymes and songs to use at home, particularly if unable or unwilling to check out library books.

The rest of the program is individual sharing time with caregivers moving around three or four displays or tables independently. One table should contain board, cloth, high-contrast, pattern, and touch-and-feel books that can be checked out. A second table can display nursery-rhyme, song, Mother Goose, and parenting books for check-out. The third table can be an activities table with ideas such as making simple homemade books or ways for the baby to touch and explore interesting textures. The tables should be in an area away from the group-time area.

FIGURE 4.1 Sample Infant Program—Number One

Opening Song:

Hel - lo ev - ery - one. How are you to - day?

I'm glad that you've come to lis - ten, dance, and play.

Share Book: *The Baby's Book of Babies* by Kathy Henderson.

Rhymes/Songs: *Finger/Hand Rhyme—Pat-A-Cake*

Pat-a-cake	*Clap baby's hands*
Pat-a-cake	
Baker's Man	
Bake me a cake	
As fast as you can.	
Roll it	*Roll baby's hands*
And pat it	*Pat hands twice*
And mark it with a "B"	*Make a "B" on baby's chest*
And put it in the oven	*Pat baby's tummy*
For baby and me.	

Toe/Foot Rhyme—Shoe the Little Horse
(Do with baby lying down on back)

Shoe the little horse	*Pat bottom of left foot*
Shoe the little mare	*Pat bottom of right foot*
Here a nail	*Gently tickle left foot*
There a nail	*Gently tickle right foot*
But pony goes bare.	*Wiggle both feet*

Tickle/Touch Rhyme—Knock on the Door

Knock on the door	*Knock on baby's forehead*
Ring the bell	*Gently push nose*
Walk right in	*Tickle fingers on baby's mouth*
Uh-oh I fell!	*Tickle fingers straight down from mouth and tickle stomach.*

Bounce/Lift Rhyme—Ride A Cock-Horse

Ride a cock-horse	*Bounce baby on knee facing you*
To Banbury Cross	
To see a fine lady	
Upon a white horse.	
With rings on her fingers	*Wiggle baby's fingers*
And bells on her toes	*Wiggle baby's toes*
She shall have music	*Bounce baby on knees again*
Wherever she goes.	

FIGURE 4.1 Continued

Share Books:	*Farm Animals* by Lucy Cousins (Board Book)
	Playtime for Baby by Susan Baum
Rhymes/Songs:	*Finger/Hand Rhyme—Hot Cross Buns*

Hot cross buns	*Hold baby's hands*
Hot cross buns	*and clap together*
One a penny	*Swing hands left*
Two a penny	*Swing hands right*
Hot cross buns.	*Clap hands together again*
If you have no daughters	*Pull hands back to chest*
Give them to your sons	*Pull hands out again*
One a penny	*Swing hands left*
Two a penny	*Swing hands right*
Hot cross buns.	*Clap hands together again*

Toe/Foot Rhyme—One Little Piggy

*Starting at little toe, wiggle each toe
in turn until you reach the big toe.*
One little piggy
Two little piggy
Three little piggy
Four.
But don't forget big piggy
That makes one more!

Tickle/Touch Rhyme—Two Little Eyes

Two little eyes	*Point to baby's eyes*
To look around	
Two little ears	*Wiggle baby's ears*
To hear each sound	
One little nose	*Wiggle baby's nose*
That smells what's sweet	
One little mouth	*Wiggle baby's mouth*
That likes to eat.	

Bounce/Lift Rhyme—Leg Over Leg

*Cross your legs and sit baby on your ankle Bounce baby to rhythm,
lift leg up on Jump OR Bounce baby on knees and lift on Jump.*
Leg over leg
Dog went to Dover
He came to a wall
Jump! He went over.

FIGURE 4.1 Continued

Song/Lullaby: *Rock-a-bye baby* (Traditional)
Rock-a-bye baby
On the tree top
When the wind blows
The cradle will rock
When the bough breaks
The cradle will fall
And down will come baby
Cradle and all.

Closing Song:

Good - bye, Good - bye, to you and you and you.

Good - bye, Good - bye, I love to be with you.

Individual Sharing Time

Display table I   Cloth, board, pattern, and high-contrast books

Display table II   Nursery rhyme, Mother Goose, song, and parenting books

Display table III   *Touch and feel station*—Baby can fingerpaint with jello, whipped cream, or baby cereal

Touch and feel station—Finger jello in plastic bag tied securely. Baby can squish and touch bag. Do not let plastic go in baby's mouth. Or have baby play with finger jello.

Touch and feel book—Show how to make a homemade touch and feel book. Use glue stick or Elmer's glue to adhere materials to cardboard pages. Hole-punch it and tie pages together with shoe strings. Materials you can use include: corrugated cardboard, aluminum foil, crepe paper, tissue paper, terry towel, bubble wrap, sponge, fake fur, ribbed corduroy, sandpaper, etc.

FIGURE 4.1 Sample Infant Program—Number Two

Opening Song:

Hel - lo ev - ery - one. How are you to - day?

I'm glad that you've come to lis - ten, dance, and play.

Share Book: *Tickle, Tickle* by Helen Oxenbury

Rhymes/Songs: *Finger/Hand Rhyme—Ten Little Fingers*
Ten little fingers
Dance and play   *Wiggle baby's fingers*
Ten little fingers
Wiggle all day.

Ten little toes
Dance and play   *Wiggle baby's toes*
Ten little toes
Wiggle all day.

Toe/Foot Rhyme—Eeny, Meeny, Miny Mo
Eeny, meeny, miny mo
Catch a piggy by his toe
If he hollers, let him go
Eeny, meeny, miny mo.

*(On first line, starting with little toe, wiggle one toe at a time
until you have wiggled all four toes. On the second and third lines,
wiggle the big toe. On the last line, wiggle your way back down
to the little toe again.)*

Tickle/Touch Rhyme—Eye Winker, Tom Tinker
Eye Winker   *Touch one eyelid gently*
Tom Tinker   *Touch other eyelid gently*
Nose Dropper   *Touch nose*
Mouth Eater   *Touch mouth*
Chin Chopper   *Touch chin*
Chin Chopper Chin   *Tickle gently under chin*

FIGURE 4.1 Continued

Bounce/Lift Rhyme—To Market, To Market
To market, to market,
To buy a fat pig;
Home again, home again
Jiggety jig.

To market, to market,
To buy a fat hog;
Home again, home again
Jiggety jog.

(Bounce baby gently on knees. You can also swing the baby while bouncing. On last line of each verse, lift baby up.)

Share Books: *Hen on the Farm* by Lucy Cousins (Cloth Book)

This Little Piggy by Moira Kemp

Rhymes/Songs: *Toe/Foot Rhyme—This Little Piggy*
This little piggy went to market
This little piggy stayed home
This little piggy had roast beef
This little piggy had none.
And this little piggy cried
Wee, wee, wee,
All the way home.

(Starting with the big toe, touch one toe at a time holding onto the toe while saying each line until reaching the last little toe. Wiggle it while saying the last two lines and gently tickle the bottom of the foot.)

Finger/Hand Rhyme—These are Baby's Fingers

These are baby's fingers	*Touch fingers*
These are baby's toes	*Touch toes*
This is baby's tummy button	*Point to belly button*
Round and round it goes.	*Make circles on tummy around belly button.*

Tickle/Touch Rhyme—Round and Round the Garden

Round and round the garden	*Make circles with your finger*
Goes the teddy bear	*on baby's palm*
One step	*Climb up arm*
Two steps	
Tickle under there!	*Tickle lightly under the arm*

FIGURE 4.1 Continued

Bounce/Lift Rhyme—Trot, Trot to Boston

Bounce baby on your knees.
On last line, open your legs and let baby fall in!
Trot, trot to Boston
Trot, trot to Lynn,
Watch out baby
Or you'll fall in!

Song/Lullaby: *Hush Little Baby* (Traditional)
Hush little baby, don't say a word,
Papa's (or Mama's) gonna buy you a mocking bird.
And if that mocking bird won't sing,
Papa's gonna buy you a diamond ring.
And if the diamond ring turns brass,
Papa's gonna buy you a looking glass.
And if that looking glass gets broke,
Papa's gonna buy you a billy goat.
And if that billy goat won't pull,
Papa's gonna buy you a cart and bull.
And if that cart and bull turn over,
Papa's gonna buy you a dog named Rover.
And if that dog named Rover won't bark,
Papa's gonna buy you a horse and cart.
And if that horse and cart fall down,
You'll still be the sweetest little baby in town.

Closing Song:

Good - bye, Good - bye, to you and you and   you.

Good - bye, Good - bye, I love to be with   you.

FIGURE 4.1 Continued

Individual Sharing Time

Display table I	Cloth, board, pattern, and high-contrast books
Display table II	Nursery rhyme, Mother Goose, song, and parenting books
Display table III	*Display Homemade Point-and-Name Book* Cut bright color poster board into equal pieces for pages of the book. Round the edges if possible instead of leaving them sharp. Punch holes and tie with shoe strings. *OR* Use an inexpensive photo album. Cut pictures from catalogs, magazines, coloring books or use photos. Make sure you use one object per page and that the objects are large and easily recognizable. If you use photos, do not forget to include one of baby.

Librarians need to remain calm and be flexible for problems that may arise. One cannot expect infants to be totally quiet or listen as preschoolers would. Older infants may attempt to crawl away from their caregiver and may be distracted easily. Some infants may even try to approach the librarian to grab the teddy bear. Some babies may cry, and if crying continues for a long period of time or is totally distracting, you may politely ask the adult to leave the circle for a few minutes and to go to another area of the room where they still can watch from a distance. Encourage them to join you again as soon as possible.

An excellent how-to-do-it resource book for infant programming is *Mother Goose Time* by Jane Marino and Dorothy Houlihan. (H.W. Wilson, 1992.) A different approach is provided in *Beginning With Books: Library Programming for Infants, Toddlers, and Preschoolers* by Nancy DeSalvo (Library Professional Publications, 1993).

TODDLER I/ CAREGIVER STORY PROGRAMS

Story programs for toddlers (those children who have progressed from crawling to walking) and their caregivers have some similarities to infant and caregiver programs, yet they are different because these children have reached a different developmental stage. Toddler I programs as defined here are for children ages one to two or 1½ to 2½. Again, these programs are basically for the caregivers: to build on what the parent already knows; to model sharing books, nursery rhymes, hand and finger rhymes, poems, creative dramatics, and songs; and to encourage caregivers to continue these activities at home. Many of the benefits of this program coincide with those of infant/caregiver programs, though there are some differences. Many toddlers will be watching and listening to the librarian, and older ones may participate in the activities in some way. They are learning that the library is a nice, pleasant place to go, and a fun place for the child and parent. This is the first step in making library visits a habit for children when they get older. Toddlers will also begin to understand what books are, how they are read (from front to back, etc.), and that reading books is an activity to be enjoyed with the caregiver. They are discovering language and increasing their listening skills. They will show more response to music and rhyme, and they begin to imitate the adult. They can learn simple concepts and basic body parts, and fine and gross motor skills are also developing.

Caregivers should participate in all activities and serve as models to their toddlers. They can either help the child act out the rhymes and actions, or act out the rhymes and actions themselves and have the child imitate them. Because toddlers do not have the fine motor skills to do finger plays as older preschoolers do, adults can help, but finger rhymes should be basic movements like opening and closing hands or motions using the whole arm. Rhymes that allow children to move their bodies are also good choices.

At this age, children are very active. Now that they can walk, they may wish to explore the room or materials you are using. Some will stay close to their caregiver, while others will want to move around and investigate. They may argue, scream, or cry if the caregiver tries to pull them back to the circle, for children of this age are beginning to show independence. If the exploring toddler is not disturbing the rest of the group, ignore him/her, because this program is more for the benefit of the caregiver. If a child is disruptive for a long period of time, you may wish to encourage the adult to take him or her out of the circle to another area of the room. The adult still can watch the activities from a distance until the child is ready to join the group again.

As in infant/caregiver programs, a Toddler I program does not need to be thematically arranged. It is more important to have a variety of short, appropriate activities with a chance for the toddlers to move often. It is also not necessary to have a series of programs. As suggested for infant programs, it is more important to try to reach more caregivers who will benefit from the program than to have a series of programs. You may wish to reach caregivers who do not normally come to the library by holding programs outside of the library. Likewise, programs should be in the early evening or on a Saturday. If programs must be held in the daytime, offer them in the morning to avoid toddler nap times.

Ten to 15 adults with toddlers is a manageable group. Two sessions back-to-back are preferable to a larger group, but if that is not possible, make sure group sharing time is short. Also make sure you have enough resource books to circulate. Adults can sit in a large semi-circle or three-quarters circle on the floor with their toddler in front of them or on their lap. The librarian sits in the front facing caregivers and children in a location where everyone can see. Make sure to have caregivers introduce themselves and their toddlers to the group.

Because children of this age are very active, plan programs accordingly. Many quick activities should be used that allow for a lot of movement. A coordinated, active rhyme or creative dramatics may follow a book on a certain subject. The sample Toddler I programs that follow are divided into two parts, like the infant programs. One part is a group sharing time of approximately 20 minutes followed by individual sharing time. The sample programs for the group sharing time consist of: 1. an opening song; 2. a book naming body parts or naming objects; 3. an active rhyme or finger game; 4. a book that will allow toddlers to make sounds, repeat a simple word, or answer simple questions; 5. creative dramatics; 6. a flannel or magnetic presentation with a few pieces or a simple puppet to use with a rhyme or song; 7. a book that will allow toddlers to act out motions; and 8. a closing song. If children are too active or inattentive, a story or activity can be left out. Make sure you keep a list of your activities near you so that you can quickly move from one activity to the next. If you have too large a time lapse, you will lose the toddlers' attention. Remember, children may try to approach you and grab your books and puppets. Keep the materials behind you or out of sight as much as possible until you need them. A sheet with nursery rhymes, simple poems, hand and finger rhymes, creative dramatics, and songs that you used with the toddlers should be provided for the adults to encourage them to continue the experience at home. If you are having one or two programs, try to include a list of additional activities than what you presented so caregivers will have more ideas to share.

During individual sharing time, three or four displays or tables should be set up for adults to move around and look at on their

FIGURE 4.2 Sample Toddler I Program—Number One

Opening Song: *(Sway or move body back and forth for the entire song. On first line, wave both hands. On second line, hold both hands out with palms up. On third line, point hand to chest to signify "I," and sway with hands on waist for last line. Repeat twice.)*

Hel - lo ev - ery - one. How are you to - day?

I'm glad that you've come for sto - ries, songs, and play.

Share Book: *Here Are My Hands* by Bill Martin *OR*
Bright Eyes, Brown Skin by Cheryl Willis Hudson and Bernette G. Ford.

Active Rhyme/Song: *Active Finger Rhyme—Put Your Finger On Your Nose*

(Sing to tune "If You're Happy and You Know It" and do actions accordingly)
Put your finger on your nose
On your nose
Put your finger on your nose
On your nose
Put your finger on your nose
But don't put it on your toes
Put your finger on your nose
on your nose.

Put your finger *on* your ear...
But don't put it *in* your ear...

Put your finger on your hair...
But don't put it in the air...

Put your finger on your hand...
But don't put it in the sand...

Put your finger on your belly...
But don't put it in the jelly...

FIGURE 4.2 Continued

Share Book:	*What Can Rabbit Hear?* by Lucy Cousins
Creative Dramatics:	*Here Is a Bunny*

(Hold hands on top of head and wave like bunny ears on first two lines. Make big circle with hands on third line. Hold hand up to ear on fourth line. Hop on fifth line. On last two lines give one big jump, then stop and bend down to ground.)
Here is a bunny
With ears so funny
And here is his hole in the ground.
When he hears a noise
He hops, hops, hops
Into his hole
Then stops, stops, stops.

Magnetic/Flannel Board Song: *Old MacDonald* (Traditional)

Use only three verses and easy sounds the child can make such as a cow mooing, a duck quacking, and a pig oinking. Provide patterns if possible for adults to take home and make. With little pieces of magnetic stripping (available at discount or craft stores) on the back, they can be fastened to the refrigerator and the adult and child can sing the song together often at home.

Book to Act Out: *Golden Bear* by Ruth Young.

Closing Song: Choice of Songs—*Goodbye Song* or *Three Bears in the Bed*

Three Bears in the Bed (Traditional)
(Roll hands on "Roll Over" lines and on last line, put head on hands and pretend to sleep.)
Three bears in the bed
And the little child said
"Roll Over, Roll Over,"
And they all rolled over
And one fell out

Two bears in the bed
And the little child said
"Roll Over, Roll Over,"
And they all rolled over
And one fell out

One bear in the bed
And the little child said

FIGURE 4.2 Continued

"Roll Over, Roll Over,"
And bear rolled over
And he fell out

No bears in the bed
And the little child said
"Good Night."

Good - bye, Good - bye, to you and you and you.

Good - bye, Good - bye, I love to be with you.

Individual Sharing Time	—Separate Room
Display table I	Board books, point-and-name books, manipulative books, touch-and-feel books, and other simple picture books that can be checked out.
Display table II	Nursery-rhyme, song, Mother Goose, poem, easy finger, hand, or movement-rhyme, and parenting books for check-out.
Display table III	Homemade puzzles—Show how to make homemade puzzles. Use coloring books, magazines, or catalogs but make sure the picture is simple. Use glue stick or Elmer's glue to adhere it to cardboard or poster board. Cover with contact paper if you wish. Cut into three or four large pieces.

FIGURE 4.2 Sample Toddler I Program—Number Two

Opening Song:

(Sway or move body back and forth for the entire song. On first line, wave both hands. On second line, hold both hands out with palms up. On third line, point hand to chest to signify "I", and sway with hands on waist for last line. Repeat twice.)

Hel - lo ev - ery - one. How are you to - day?

I'm glad that you've come for sto - ries, songs, and play.

Share Book:

My Pet by Noelle Carter

Active Rhyme/Song:

Active Rhyme—Up The Hill
Here goes turtle up the hill
Creepy, creepy, creepy, creepy.
Here goes a rabbit up the hill
Boing, boing, boing, boing.
Here goes an elephant up the hill
Thud, thud, thud, thud.
Here goes a snake up the hill
Slither, slither, slither, slither.
Here comes a rock down the hill
Boom, boom, boom, boom, crash!

(You may act this out by making motions suggested in every second line OR have adult use fingers starting at toddler's palm, and crawling up the shoulder each time in a manner suggested by the words. On last line the rock (adult fist) goes booming down the hill and crashes in toddler's palm.)

Share Book:

Where's Spot? by Eric Hill

Creative Dramatics:

Little Puppy
A little puppy went out to play
Over the hills and far away.
Mommy Dog said Bow-Wow, Bow-Wow,
And puppy came back, wagging his tail.

(Bend over with knees and palms on floor like a puppy. Sway body to rhyme. For Mommy Dog, sit up with knees still on floor, but hands held in front of body like paws. On last line, revert to original position and shake back end.)

FIGURE 4.2 Continued

Puppet and Song:	*How Much Is That Doggie in the Window* (Traditional)
	(Use a puppy puppet OR make a paper plate doggie puppet for each child using a small paper plate attached to a tongue depressor for a handle and with a doggie face and ears. Either way, have toddlers make "woof" sound with you.)

How much is that doggie in the window? (*Woof-Woof*)
The one with the waggily tail. (*Woof-Woof*)
How much is that doggie in the window? (*Woof-Woof*)
I do hope that doggie's for sale. (*Woof-Woof*)

I don't want a or bunny or a kitten. (*Woof-Woof*)
I don't want a parrot that talks. (*Woof-Woof*)
I don't want a bowl of little fishies. (*Woof-Woof*)
I can't take a goldfish for walks. (*Woof-Woof*)

Repeat first verse.

Book to Act Out:	*This Little Baby's Playtime* by Lynn Breeze.
Closing Song:	Choice of Songs—*Goodbye Song* or *Twinkle, Twinkle, Little Star*

Twinkle, Twinkle, Little Star (Traditional)
Twinkle, twinkle, little star,
How I wonder what you are.
Up above the world so high,
Like a diamond in the sky,
Twinkle, twinkle, little star
How I wonder what you are.

In the dark blue sky you keep,
And often through my curtains peep.
For you never shut your eye,
'Til the sun is in the sky,
Twinkle, twinkle, little star,
How I wonder what you are.

[Can wave star back and forth along with music. Have one for each child. Yellow construction paper star with glitter (if desired) fastened to a straw.]

Individual Sharing Time	*—Separate Room*
Display table I	Board books, point-and-name books, manipulative books, touch-and-feel books, and other simple picture books that can be checked out.
Display table II	Nursery-rhyme, song, Mother Goose, poem, easy finger, hand, or movement-rhyme, and parenting books for check-out.

FIGURE 4.2 Continued

Display table III	Toddler's First Art—Have large pieces of cardboard or poster board cut into squares. Have the adult use masking tape to tape the edges of the cardboard down on the floor in front of child so that the cardboard does not move. Provide large crayons for child to color her/his first work of art! You can also use masking tape or a rubber band to hold three large crayons together so toddler can scribble several colors at the same time. Provide magnetic stripping if you wish so the adult can fasten the art to the refrigerator at home.

own. One table should contain board books, point-and-name books, manipulative books, touch-and-feel books, and other simple picture books that can be checked out. A second table should display nursery-rhyme, song, Mother Goose, poem, and parenting books for circulation. The third table should be an activities table. This can contain ideas for making simple homemade books, puzzles, or art activities appropriate for the toddlers' developmental level. The tables should be in a location away from the group sharing area. Make sure you remind caregivers to share books, rhymes, poems, creative dramatics, songs, and learning activities at home.

Resource books that may also help in planning Toddler I programs include: *Mother Goose Time* by Jane Marino and Dorothy Houlihan (H.W. Wilson, 1992); *Beginning With Books: Library Programming for Infants, Toddlers, and Preschoolers* by Nancy DeSalvo (Library Professional Publications, 1993); and *Early Childhood Literature Sharing Programs in Libraries* by Ann Carlson (Library Professional Publications, 1985).

TODDLER II/ CAREGIVER STORY PROGRAMS

Story programs for this age group are directed to both the toddlers and their caregivers. Most toddlers will experience one of their first group storytime experiences in which they will be more actively involved in creative dramatics, rhymes, and songs and may listen more intently while the librarian shares stories. For caregivers, this how-to-do it program builds on the knowledge they may already have on reading to their young child, sharing language, songs, and art activities. The librarian also models to the adult the way to read to young children and share learning activities at home. The age span for children attending this program is two to three years or 2½ to 3½.

Benefits for toddlers include learning what books are; how books are read (including directionality, etc.); how to handle and respect books; and that reading books is important. Other advantages are that toddlers are learning language; listening skills; basic concepts; how to respond to music and rhyme; simple fine and gross motor skills; how to imitate caregivers; and that the library is a nice, fun place to go, which may become a regular habit when the child becomes older. Caregivers learn how to share books, nursery rhymes, simple poems, hand and finger rhymes, creative dramatics, and songs with their toddlers and will be encouraged to do the same at home with their child. Caregivers should participate in all activities and serve as models to their toddlers by either helping the child act out rhymes and actions or acting them out themselves and having the child imitate them. Older toddlers can do slightly more complex finger plays but still do not have the fine motor skills like more advanced preschoolers, so adults should help. However, finger rhymes chosen should also be basic movements like opening and closing hands or pointing to various fingers in count-down rhymes.

Children at this age are still very active. Some will explore the room while others will stay close to their caregiver. As with younger toddlers, some children may become disruptive and adults may need to take them away from the area for a short time. Other children may lie down and not seem to watch anything going on. First, do not assume a child is not soaking in some of the experience. Many caregivers will frustratingly tell librarians that their child does not seem to be listening, though later at home the child will sing part of a song that has been presented before the caregiver has had a chance to practice it with the child. Also, even if the child does not appear to be listening, he or she is enjoying the storytime experience in his or her own way. Caregivers can reinforce what is being presented by repeating it at home.

Toddler II programs are usually thematically arranged, though that is not necessary. It is more important to have a variety of short activities that allow active toddlers much movement. Also, if you do select a theme, make sure that every item related to the theme is developmentally appropriate for toddlers. Zealous planners occasionally are so concerned about choosing items to fit a certain theme that they often forget that certain activities might be more appropriate for preschoolers than toddlers.

Most libraries today hold a series of Toddler II programs. If you do have a series, you probably will want to hold it for at least six weeks, because it takes that long for most children to become adjusted to the storytime experience. Again, however, that is not possible for every library. Holding a few programs that reach more people who can benefit from the experience is more vital than holding a series for those caregivers who already know the importance of reading and sharing language with their children. Programs should also be held in the early evening hours or on a Saturday for working caregivers. If offered in the daytime, avoid afternoon nap times.

Toddler II programs are similar to Toddler I in the respect that the group should be limited to ten to 15 adults with toddlers. More than this in one session will require group sharing time to be shortened. Two sessions back-to-back are a possibility, but it is necessary to have enough resource books for check-out. Children sit in front of their caregiver or on their lap in a large semi-circle or three-quarters circle. The librarian is in front on the floor or on a very low stool facing the caregivers and children. It is important that everyone can see you.

This program, like those described previously, is divided into two parts. One part, group sharing time, can last slightly longer than in a Toddler I program. Aim for 25 minutes, but be prepared to cut some activities if the group is too restless. Two sample Toddler II programs follow, one having a transportation theme and the other a bear storytime. The sample programs consist of: 1. an opening song or finger rhyme; 2. a story; 3. an active rhyme, finger rhyme, creative dramatics, or song with motions; 4. a second story; 5. a second active rhyme, finger rhyme, creative dramatics, or song with motions; 6. a third story; 7. a third active rhyme, finger rhyme, creative dramatics, or song with motions; and 8. a closing song. It is important that the adult participate with the child by singing and making motions or helping the child make the motions. If you are having a series of toddler programs, repeat the same opening and closing rhyme/song each week. Also, try to repeat some activities from week to week. Keep a list of activities near you so that the program moves quickly. Any lag could prove disastrous. Toddlers may want to hold the books or puppets that you are using, so try to keep them behind you or out of sight when not in use. If you are having a series of programs, provide a name tag for each child and caregiver if possible. If not, make sure the caregivers introduce themselves and their child each session. Provide a sheet with nursery rhymes, simple poems, hand and finger rhymes, creative dramatics, and songs that you used for the program for adults to take along and share the experience at home.

FIGURE 4.3 Sample Toddler II Program—Transportation

Opening Song:

Good Time Bus

1. Climb right up on the Good Time Bus, Climb right up on the Good Time Bus,

Climb right up on the Good Time Bus, And come a - long with us.

1. Climb right up on the Good Time Bus,
   Climb right up on the Good Time Bus,
   Climb right up on the Good Time Bus,
   And come along with us.
   (March in place.)

2. Chug, chug, chug goes the Good Time Bus,
   Chug, chug, chug goes the Good Time Bus,
   Chug, chug, chug goes the Good Time Bus,
   So come along with us.
   (Two fists, held close together at waist level, fingers pointing down, move up and down.)

3. Steer, steer, steer on the Good Time Bus,
   Steer, steer, steer on the Good Time Bus,
   Steer, steer, steer on the Good Time Bus,
   And come along with us.
   (Make steering motions.)

4. Up the hill goes the Good Time Bus,
   Up the hill goes the Good Time Bus,
   Up the hill goes the Good Time Bus,
   So come along with us.
   (Move hands as if going up hill and stand on tip toes.)

5. Down the hill goes the Good Time Bus,
   Down the hill goes the Good Time Bus,
   Down the hill goes the Good Time Bus,
   So come along with us.
   (Move body slowly down to floor in time to music.)

FIGURE 4.3 Continued

Share Book: *Freight Train* by Donald Crews

Finger Rhyme: *Choo, Choo, Choo*

*(Run fingers up one arm to shoulder,
then run them down again. Make train sounds.)*
Choo, choo, choo, choo,
A train runs up the track.
Whoo, whoo, whoo, whoo,
Hear it now, coming back!

Song With Motions: *Down by the Station* (Traditional)

*(Make fists and move arms in a circular fashion like wheels of a train for
the first four lines. On fifth line, bring up one hand and shade eyes as
if looking, then pull handle. Thump fists for puff, puff and then pull handle
again for toot, toot and then move again as at beginning.)*
Down by the station
Early in the morning,
See the little puffer bellies
Standing in a row.
See the engine driver
Pull the little handle,
Puff puff, toot toot,
Off we go!

Share Book: *Flying* by Donald Crews

Creative Dramatics: *The Airplane.*

*(Hold arms out straight from body and move up and down
like an airplane. Move as called for in rhyme.)*
See the airplane
Flying way up high.
As it tips its wings
See it go by.

The plane goes up
The plane goes down.
The plane flies high
All over the town.

Share Story: *The Wheels on the Bus* by Paul Zelinsky

FIGURE 4.3 Continued

Song With Motions:	*Wheels of the Bus* (Traditional)
	(Make fists and move arms in a circular fashion like the wheels of a bus) The wheels of the bus go round and round, Round and round, round and round. The wheels of the bus go round and round All through the town.
	(Make fist and beep horn up and down) The horn on the bus goes beep, beep, beep, Beep, beep, beep, beep, beep, beep, The horn on the bus goes beep, beep, beep, All through the town.
	(Palms facing out, move arms back and forth like wipers) The wipers on the bus go swish, swish, swish, Swish, swish, swish, swish, swish, swish, The wipers on the bus go swish, swish, swish, All through the town.
	(Child bumps up and down by self or on adult's lap or adult lifts child up and down) The people on the bus go up and down, Up and down, up and down, The people on the bus go up and down, All through the town.
Closing Song:	*Good Time Bus*
	Repeat Opening Song but add last verse- Wave goodbye on the Good Time Bus, Wave goodbye on the Good Time Bus, Wave goodbye on the Good Time Bus, And come along with us.
Individual Sharing Time	—Separate Room
Display table I	Simple books appropriate for this age including participation stories, stories in rhyme, stories that are songs, easy concept books, informational books, etc. that can be checked out.
Display table II	Song, poem, easy finger play or rhyme books, learning—activity books. and parenting books for check-out.
Display table III	Since *Freight Train* stresses colors, make the activity table an art activity related to colors. Have caregivers make a homemade color book. White

FIGURE 4.3 Continued	

construction paper can be paper punched and tied with yarn. Have the caregiver label a color on each page and then have the child color that page with the appropriate large color. Rubber band or masking tape two or three colors together and have the child make some rainbow pages too! The book can be labeled "My Color Book."

Or make a homemade train/color book. Have poster board train shapes (cut from cookie cutter). Make sure each adult gets one. Adults can trace the train and cut several out of different colors of construction paper. Glue on to book pages, labeling colors. Child can identify colors.

Sample Toddler II Program—Bears

Opening Finger Game:

Right Hand, Left Hand
This is my right hand
I'll raise it up high.
This is my left hand
I'll touch the sky.
Right hand, left hand,
Roll them around.
Left hand, right hand,
Pound, pound, pound.

(Have caregiver raise toddler's hands at appropriate time and help toddler roll and pound hands.)

Share Book:

Goldilocks and the Three Bears by Penny Ives

Creative Dramatics:

Goldilocks

(Have toddlers with caregivers' help act out the part of Goldilocks. Walk (in place) to an imaginary door. Hold hand over eyes to look in the window. Open the door. Walk in. Try the large, medium and small bowl of porridge with an imaginary spoon and eat the contents of the small bowl. Try the large chair (rock body back and forth in place like on a rocking chair), middle-size chair, and small chair. Rock on it until it breaks. Try beds by laying head on hands. When the three bears return home, Goldilocks jumps out the window. Close by saying "Goldilocks never returned to the house of the three bears.")

Share Book:

Teddy Bear Teddy Bear by Michael Hague

Active Rhyme:

Teddy Bear Teddy Bear

(Act out the story just read. Motions are in the back of the book. If you are uncomfortable using the line "Say your prayers," use "Brush your hair" instead.)

FIGURE 4.3 Continued

Share Story: *How Do I Put It On?* by Shigeo Watanabe

You may wish to read this story twice. The first time share the book, and the second time, holding a teddy bear, dress it in the manner described in the book.

Song With Motions: *The Bear Went Up the Mountain* (Traditional)

(There are several ways to use this song with toddlers. They can slap their knees while the bear goes up and down the mountain, or they can climb their hands slowly up and down in the air, or even march in place up and down the mountain. For the spoken line and verse saying ''the other side of the mountain,'' place hand over eyes pretending to see what is on the other side of the mountain.)
The bear went up the mountain
The bear went up the mountain
The bear went up the mountain
To see what he could see.

And what do you think he saw? *(spoken)*

The other side of the mountain
The other side of the mountain
The other side of the mountain
Is all that he did see.

So the bear went down the mountain
The bear went down the mountain
The bear went down the mountain
Very happily.

Closing Song: *Five Bears in the Bed* (Traditional)

(Toddlers can not put one finger down at a time to show the number of bears. You may wish to make a flannel or magnetic board story of this song to show the number of bears remaining. Have children roll hands on ''Roll Over'' lines and they can pretend to fall out of the bed at the end of each line. On the last line, wave good night.)
Five bears in the bed
And the little child said
''Roll Over, Roll Over,''
And they all rolled over
And one fell out...

Four bears in the bed...

Three bears in the bed...

Two bears in the bed...

FIGURE 4.3 Continued

	One bear in the bed And the little child said "Roll Over, Roll Over," And bear rolled over And he fell out
	No bears in the bed And the little child said "Good Night."
Individual Sharing Time	—Separate Room
Display table I	Simple books appropriate for this age including participation stories, stories in rhyme, stories that are songs, easy concept books, and informational books, etc. that can be checked out.
Display table II	Song, poem, easy finger play or rhyme books, learning-activity books and parenting books for check-out.
Display table III	*Homemade Musical Instruments* Find a recording of the song *Teddy Bears' Picnic,* written by Jimmy Kennedy. Play it on a cassette recorder at the third table. Have several homemade musical instruments available so that caregivers will see how to make such instruments. Have children play these along with the teddy bear song. Examples of homemade instruments include: a coffee-can drum; two wooden spoons to hit together as sticks; an empty margarine container filled with beans with the lid securely fastened with masking tape to use as a shaker; a wooden salad-bowl drum played with a wooden spoon; plastic containers with tight lids filled with rice; two metal pan lids clapped together for cymbals, etc.

If you are having just one program, try to include more activities than what you presented so caregivers will have more ideas of rhymes and songs that are developmentally appropriate.

Individual sharing time follows the group storytime experience. Three or four displays or tables are arranged in another area for adults to browse on their own. One table should contain simple picture books, easy concept and informational books that can be checked out. A second table can contain song, poem, easy fingerplay or rhyme, learning-activity, and parenting books for checkout. The third table should be an art or learning-activities table with materials suitable to toddlers' developmental stage. Examples of art experiences that relate to the theme programs are given at the end of the sample programs.

Several resource books helpful in planning Toddler II programs include: *Storytimes for Two-Year-Olds* by Judy Nichols (American Library Association, 1987); *Beginning With Books: Library Programming for Infants, Toddlers, and Preschoolers* by Nancy DeSalvo (Library Professional Publications, 1993); and Ann Carlson's *Early Childhood Literature Sharing Programs in Libraries* (Library Professional Publications, 1985).

PRESCHOOL/ CAREGIVER STORY PROGRAMS

As stated earlier, preschool programs are the most common storytime program in libraries and are more frequently attended by a child without the caregiver participating in the program or even being in the same area. The advantages of having a caregiver present have been listed previously, and more libraries should give consideration to having preschool/caregiver programs or family storytime programs.

Benefits for this type of program are similar to those expressed for other age groups: preschoolers are discovering that books are enjoyable; they are developing reading-readiness skills that will be beneficial to them when they begin to read; they are learning language, listening skills, and basic concepts; they are enjoying music and rhyme; their fine and gross motor skills are developing; and they also are finding that going to the library is enjoyable, which may become a regular habit when they become older. As in toddler programs, caregivers are learning how to share books enthusiastically, how to encourage children's verbal reactions to stories, and how to share poems, finger rhymes, creative dramatics, and songs with their preschoolers.

Preschool programs are almost always thematically arranged and are held in series. However, why offer a lengthy series or year-round preschool storytimes if it means limiting programs for children of other ages? If this has been the habit for years, there may be complaints about cutting the number of programs specifically for preschoolers. Explain that the library feels it is important to program to children of all ages rather than just a few, and that it is the library's goal to reach more caregivers of preschoolers.

Programs should be held in the early evening if possible or on a Saturday. Daytime programs are also a possibility, including afternoons, but be conscious of the working hours of caregivers or the hours public transportation operates in your area.

More children can attend preschool storytimes than programs held for younger children. Probably the maximum you will want at one time will be 20 to 25 children with their caregivers. Caregivers can sit behind their children with the preschoolers up front, but make sure all preschoolers can see and are not blocked by adults. Programs may last up to 45 minutes including group time, individual sharing time, and optional art activity.

Two sample preschool programs follow, one on farms and farm animals, the other on insects and spiders. The sample programs consist of: 1. an opening finger rhyme or song; 2. a story; 3. one or two active rhymes, finger rhymes, creative dramatics, poems, or songs; 4. another story; 5. one or two active rhymes, finger rhymes, creative dramatics, poems, or songs; 6. a third story; 7. another active rhyme, finger rhyme, creative dramatics, poem, or song; 8. a fourth story; and 9. a closing rhyme or song. If children are restless, you may wish to skip a story and do more active rhymes, creative dramatics, or songs. Have adults participate in songs and rhymes with the children.

Individual sharing time follows the group storytime experience. Display new picture books, easy concept and informational books, and audiocassettes appealing to preschoolers. Another table should contain books of interest to adults, including song, poem, finger-play, rhyme, learning-activity, and parenting books for check-out.

An optional art activity for each preschool program is also included. Many libraries have crafts as part of their preschool storytimes. It is important to remember that if one wishes to engage children in crafts, rather than art projects per se, that the crafts should not include precut items to be pasted or coloring sheets. Such crafts only allow children to follow the librarian's directions, a questionable learning activity that certainly can be taught in other ways. Many children are frustrated or experience a loss of self-esteem if they have difficulty following directions or if their project does not look like the librarian-made model. Instead, children should be engaged in actual art activities where they have a chance to be creative and where the whole group does not have to do an activity the same way. Children need a chance to explore different art mediums or materials with no product goal in mind. Though they will end up with a product, the process of creating it should be up to each child.

FIGURE 4.4 Sample Preschool Program—Farm and Farm Animals

Opening Finger Rhyme/Song:	*Busy Fingers*
	This is the way my fingers stand, Fingers stand, fingers stand, This is the way my fingers stand, So early in the evening. (morning)
	This is the way they dance about, Dance about, dance about, This is the way they dance about, So early in the evening. (morning)
	This is the way I fold my hands, Fold my hands, fold my hands, This is the way I fold my hands, So early in the evening. (morning)
	This is the way they go to rest, Go to rest, go to rest, This is the way they go to rest, So early in the evening. (morning)
	(Sing to tune "Here we go round the Mulberry Bush.")
Share Book:	*When the Rooster Crowed* by Patricia Lillie
Poem:	"The Rooster" —Anonymous from the book *On the Farm* (Poems selected by Lee Bennett Hopkins)
	(Read the poem twice and have children "cock-a-doodle-doo" with you the second time through.)
Share Book:	*Sitting on the Farm* by Bob King
	(Though this book has music in the back and can be sung, it is also a good story to rap due to the repetitious beat and rhyme present. Have children clap their hands or slap their knees.)
Participation Song:	*Down on Grandpa's Farm* (Raffi)
	(This song is recorded on Raffi's cassette tape "One Light, One Sun" and also is included in his book, The Second Raffi Songbook. The children participate by making the sounds of various farm animals including a cow, a hen, a sheep, a dog, and a horse. Have them stand up and act like the animals.)
Nursery Rhymes:	There are several nursery rhymes with farm themes or farm animals. Some can be acted out or used as finger rhymes.

FIGURE 4.4 Continued

Little Boy Blue
Little Boy Blue
Come blow your horn.   *(pretend to blow horn)*
The sheep are in the meadow   *(right arm gestures right)*
The cow in is the corn.   *(left arm gestures left)*
Where is the little boy
Who looks after the sheep?   *(hand over eyes—look)*
He's under the haystack
Fast asleep.   *(head rests on hands)*
Will you wake him?
No, not I.   *(shake head ''no'')*
For if I do, he'll surely cry!   *(pretend to cry)*

Baa, Baa, Black Sheep
Baa, baa, black sheep,
Have you any wool?   *(Hold hands out, palms up)*
Yes sir, yes sir,   *(Shake head ''yes'')*
Three bags full.   *(Hold up three fingers)*
One for the master,   *(Point to one finger)*
One for the dame,   *(Point to another)*
And one for the little boy   *(Point to last finger)*
Who lives down the lane.   *(Point ''down lane'')*

Little Bo Peep
Little Bo Peep
Has lost her sheep   *(Wiggle fingers)*
And doesn't know
Where to find them.   *(Hide fingers behind back)*
Leave them alone
And they will come home
Wagging their tails   *(Holding hands behind*
Behind them!   *back, wag like tails)*

Mary Had a Little Lamb   *(Sing)*
Mary had a little lamb,
Little lamb, little lamb,
Mary had a little lamb,
Its fleece was white as snow.

And everywhere that Mary went,
Mary went, Mary went,
And everywhere that Mary went,
The lamb was sure to go.

FIGURE 4.4 Continued

Share Story/Song:	*Old MacDonald* by Glen Rounds *OR* *Cat Goes Fiddle-i-Fee* by Paul Galdone *OR* *Fiddle-i-Fee* by Melissa Sweet
	(For either book, share the story first and then read it a second time having children make the sound of the various animals. All are successful with paper-bag puppets or as a clothesline story, with children pining up the animal pieces with clothespins. Another option is to use magnetic or flannel board pieces.)
Share Story:	*Big Red Barn* by Margaret Wise Brown
Closing Song:	*The More We Get Together* The more we get together, Together, together, The more we get together, The happier we'll be. For your friends are my friends, And my friends are your friends, The more we get together, The happier we'll be.
	(Place hands on waist and swing back and forth to the music. Point to someone else for "your friends" and to yourself for "my friends." Sway again on the last two lines. Music for this song is in Tom Glazer's *Eye Winker, Tom Tinker, Chin Chopper*.)

Optional Group Art Activity

Share story:	*Color Farm* by Lois Ehlert
	(Have cardboard patterns of the shapes presented in the book and provide children with large pieces of paper and crayons. Allow them to trace the various shapes they want and try to make animals on their own.)
Display Tables	—Separate Room
Display table I	A variety of books appropriate for this age group including participation stories, cumulative tales, fairy and folk tales, stories in rhyme, stories that are songs, easy concept books, easy riddles, simple poetry, informational books, etc. that can be checked out.
Display table II	Song, poem, finger play and rhyme books, learning-activity books, and parenting books for check-out.

FIGURE 4.4 Sample Preschool Program—Insect and Spiders

Opening Finger Play:	*Ten Little Fingers*	
	I have ten little fingers,	*(suit actions to words)*
	And they all belong to me.	
	I can make them do things,	
	Would you like to see?	
	I can shut them up tight,	
	Or open them up wide.	
	I can put them all together,	
	Or make them all hide.	
	I can make them jump high,	
	I can make them jump low,	
	I can fold them together,	
	And hold them just so.	*(fold in lap)*

Introduce Theme: Share with the children why a spider is not an insect. Insects have six legs (three pair) and if winged, four wings (two pair). Examples of insects are bees, wasps, butterflies, moths, flies, dragonflies, fireflies, ladybugs, beetles, grasshoppers, crickets, mosquitoes, and ants. A spider has eight legs (four pair) and no wings. Have children name some insects. You may wish to share a big book depicting different insects such as *Fascinating Insects* from the *Giant Step Picture Library* available from Educational Insights Incorp., Dominguez Hills, CA, 1992. Another choice is the book *Insects and Crawly Creatures,* from the *Eye Openers* series by Dorling Kindersley, publisher. Or you may wish to display flannel or magnetic pieces of different common insects on a flannel or magnetic board.

Share Book: *Very Hungry Caterpillar* by Eric Carle *OR*
Caterpillar and the Polliwog by Jack Kent

(You may wish to use the Folkmanis puppet of the caterpillar that turns into a butterfly. Folkmanis Puppet Headquarters are in Emeryville, Calif.)

Fingerplay:	*Fuzzy Wuzzy Caterpillar*	
	Fuzzy wuzzy caterpillar	*(Make fist except for index finger)*
	Crawling all around.	*(Finger makes crawling motion)*
	Fuzzy wuzzy caterpillar	
	Curls up on the ground.	*(Curl finger into fist.)*
	Spins himself a blanket	*(Spinning motion with hands)*
	And covers up his head.	*(Hands cover head)*
	Falls fast asleep	*(Head on palms of hands)*
	In his silken bed.	
	Fuzzy wuzzy caterpillar	
	Wakes up by and by.	*(Pretend to wake up)*
	Now he has lovely wings	*(Flap hands)*
	For he's a butterfly!	

FIGURE 4.4 Continued

Participation Story:	*Old Black Fly* by Jim Aylesworth *OR* *You Can't Catch Me* by Joanne Oppenheim *(In the first story, children can join in the refrain "Shoo fly! Shoo fly! Shooo! In the second book, children can join in the refrain "You can't catch me.")*
Participation Song:	*I Know an Old Lady Who Swallowed a Fly* *(You can use the book by Glen Rounds or a handmade puppet or the "Old Lady" puppet by Nancy Renfro Studios, Austin, Texas. This also lends itself well to a magnetic or flannel board presentation.)*
Active Song:	*Baby Bumble Bee* *(Sing to "Turkey in the Straw")* Oh I'm bringing home a baby bumble bee. Won't my Momma be so proud of me. Oh I'm bringing home a baby bumble bee. Ouch! He stung me! (Have children stand up and sing along with this song to stretch. Sing the song at least three times. The first time clap along with the music. The second time through, stamp your feet. The third time, clap hands and stamp feet. For each verse on the last line, stop action, and throw up hands for "Ouch!" and then shake fists for "He stung me" finishing with a buzzing sound.)

Finger play:

Bees

Here is the beehive,	*(Hold up fist tightly closed)*
But where are the bees?	
Hidden away	*(Hold other hand over fist)*
So nobody sees.	
Soon they'll come	
Creeping out of the hive.	
One, two, three, four, five!	*(Open fingers one by one)*
Buzzzzzzzzzzz!	*(Wiggle fingers)*

Participation Story: *Very Busy Spider* by Eric Carle

Nursery Rhyme:

Little Miss Muffet

Little Miss Muffet	*(Left hand fist, thumb extended)*
Sat on a tuffet	
Eating her curds and whey.	*(Eating motion with right hand)*
Along came a spider	*(Right hand walks like spider)*
And sat down beside her,	*(Right hand near left fist)*
And frightened Miss Muffet away.	*(Fist runs behind back)*

FIGURE 4.4 Continued

Song:	*Eensy, Weensy Spider*	
	The eensy, weensy spider	*(Fingers on one hand crawl*
	Climbed up the water spout.	*like a spider)*
	Down came the rain	*(Both hands sweep down)*
	And washed the spider out.	*(Swing hands back and forth)*
	Out came the sun	*(Hands overhead like sun)*
	And dried up all the rain.	*(Hands come down to side)*
	The eensy, weensy spider	*(Crawl hand up again)*
	Climbed up the spout again.	

Closing Song: *The More We Get Together* (Traditional)
The more we get together,
Together, together,
The more we get together,
The happier we'll be.
For your friends are my friends,
And my friends are your friends,
The more we get together,
  The happier we'll be.

(Place hands on waist and swing back and forth to the music. Point to someone else for "your friends" and to yourself for "my friends." Sway again on the last two lines.)

Optional Group Art Activity— Making butterflies—Have butterfly shapes precut. Put a small amount of glue in several empty margarine containers. Children can use popsicle sticks or cotton swabs to apply glue. Have sequins, beads, snippets of lace, rickrack, glitter, small pieces of ripped tissue paper, markers, etc. for children to use to decorate their butterfly. When finished, glue butterfly to a clothespin with part of the clothespin above the butterfly. You can use a small piece of chenille wrapped around the top of the clothespin for antennae.

Display Tables —Separate Room

Display table I A variety of books appropriate for this age group including participation stories, cumulative tales, fairy and folk tales, stories in rhyme, stories that are songs, easy concept books, easy riddles, simple poetry, informational books, etc. that can be checked out.

Display table II Song, poem, finger play and rhyme books, learning-activity books and parenting books for check-out.

POSITIVE REWARDS FOR ALL CAREGIVER/ CHILD STORY PROGRAMS

You may wish to give each child who attends a storytime program or series of programs a certificate for attendance. Many caregivers will be proud that their child attended such a event and will want to display the certificate or keep it for the child in a scrapbook.

Another benefit of story programs is that many caregivers will form bonds with other caregivers (particularly if you have a series of programs) and sometimes playgroups form from the library experience. Other times children become playmates and go to each other's houses, or caregivers and children may go to lunch together after a program. Children and caregivers often become friends from a library experience.

Having caregivers present is also an advantage for librarians. Particularly with active toddlers, a librarian may have a difficult time managing the group alone. Having caregivers present makes the experience not only easier to handle, but more rewarding to the child. Caregivers can redirect wandering attention and involve the child enthusiastically in creative dramatics, active times, and songs. A good rapport can be established between these caregivers and the librarian, which makes caregivers more comfortable when seeking help or asking questions of the librarian at a later date.

Finally, having programs that require caregivers and children to share time together (unlike preschool storytimes commonly held where children are alone), allows for a fairly quiet, safe environment, and a quality experience that caregivers need with their young children. Many caregivers work and children are watched at day care or preschool, or caregivers are faced with a barrage of economic and social problems and finding time to share language experiences with their child may not be their top priority. By providing this outlet, librarians are encouraging caregivers to replicate this experience at home and return to the library for more visits, which is helpful for young children's emergent literacy skills.

EVALUATION OF STORYTIME PROGRAMS

You will want to evaluate your story program, particularly if you are offering a new program. A simple check-off sheet (do not expect caregivers to write long comments) is satisfactory, or you may wish to verbally question some caregivers on whether the program helped them to continue to read, use rhymes, and sing with their children at home. Some questions asked can be: What did they enjoy most about the program? What did the child enjoy most? In what ways could the program be improved? Did the program aid in selecting materials to use or share with the child? Did the program help with ideas on how to read to the child and how to share rhymes, songs, and art activities? Was the program offered at a good time?

If you are doing the program outside of the library at a social-service agency or other site, get feedback from others at the agency. Even better, talk to or send a card to caregivers six months after the program. Ask questions such as: Are they still reading to their child and using rhymes, poems, and songs at home? Are they more interested in sharing literature, and is their child more interested in literature being read? Did they come to the library before the program was offered? Are they coming to the library now for materials? How often? Would they recommend the program to a friend? And, what other programs could the library offer that would help them with their child's literacy skills as the child is getting older?

RESOURCES TO HELP WITH PROGRAM PLANNING

RESOURCES FOR LIBRARIANS WHO SERVE YOUNG CHILDREN

Book/Materials Selection

Choosing the Best in Children's Videos. Chicago: American Library Association, 1990 (videocassette).

Friedes, Harriet. *Preschool Resource Guide: Educating and Entertaining Children Aged Two Through Five.* New York: Insight, 1993.

Jarnow, Jill. *All Ears: How to Choose and Use Recorded Music for Children.* New York: Penguin, 1991.

Lima, Carolyn. *A to Zoo: Subject Access to Children's Picture Books.* 4th ed. New York: R.R. Bowker, 1993.

Thomas, James. *Play, Learn and Grow.* New York: R. R. Bowker, 1992.

Winkel, Lois, and Sue Kimmel. *Mother Goose Comes First.* New York: Henry Holt, 1990.

Journals (Useful for Programming and General Interest)

Booklinks.
Booklist.
Building Blocks Newspaper.
Bulletin for the Center of Children's Books.
Copycat.
Five Owls.
Horn Book.
Journal of Youth Services in Libraries.
Kidstuff.
Kirkus.
Parents Choice.
Pre-K Today.
The Preschool Mailbox.
School Library Journal.
Totline.
Young Children.

Planning Programs for Caregivers and Teachers

Preschool Services and Parent Education Committee. *First Steps to Literacy.* Chicago: American Library Association, 1990.

Nespeca, Sue McCleaf. *Library Programming for Families with Young Children.* New York: Neal-Schuman, 1994.

Planning Infant/Toddler Story Programs

Carlson, Ann D. *Early Childhood Literature Sharing Programs in Libraries.* Hamden: Library Professional Publications, 1985.

DeSalvo, Nancy. *Beginning With Books.* Hamden: Library Professional Publications, 1993.

Greene, Ellin. *Books, Babies and Libraries.* Chicago: American Library Association, 1991.

Marino, Jane, and Dorothy F Houlihan. *Mother Goose Time.* New York: H.W. Wilson, 1992.

Nespeca, Sue McCleaf. *Library Programming for Families With Young Children.* New York: Neal-Schuman, 1994.

Nichols, Judy. *Storytime for Two-Year-Olds.* Chicago: American Library Association, 1987.

**General Activity Books to Expand Literature
For Infant/Toddler Story Programs**

Cohen, Lynn. *Me and My World: Young Children Explore Their World Through Art, Music, and Movement.* Palo Alto, Calif.: Monday Morning, 1986.

Haas, Carolyn Buhai. *Look At Me! Activities for Babies and Toddlers.* Glencoe, Ill.: CBH Publishing, 1985.

Miller, Karen. *Things to Do with Toddlers and Twos.* Marshfield, Mass.: Telshare, 1984. Also, *More Things to Do with Toddlers and Twos.*

Marzollo, Jean. *Supertot: Creative Learning Activities for Children From One to Three and Sympathetic Advice for Their Parents.* New York: HarperCollins, 1977.

Silberg, Jackie. *Games to Play with Babies.* Rev. ed. Mt. Rainier, Md.: Gryphon, 1993. Also, *Games to Play with Toddlers.*

Warren, Jean. *Toddler Theme-A-Saurus.* Everett, Wash.: Warren, 1991. Also, *Nursery Rhyme Theme-A-Saurus.*

Planning Preschool Story Programs

Baker, Augusta. *Storytelling Art and Technique.* New York: R.R. Bowker, 1987.

Bauer, Caroline Feller. *Caroline Feller Bauer's New Handbook for Storytellers.* Chicago: American Library Association, 1993.

Bauer, Caroline Feller. *Handbook for Storytellers.* Chicago: American Library Association, 1977.

Carlson, Ann D. *Preschooler and the Library.* Metuchen, N.J.: Scarecrow Press, 1991.

Cullum, Carolyn. *Storytime Sourcebook.* New York: Neal-Schuman, 1990.

Herb, Steven and Sara Willoughby-Herb. *Using Children's Books in Preschool Settings: A How-To-Do-It Manual.* New York: Neal-Schuman, 1994.

Irving, Jan. *Mudluscious.* Englewood, CO.: Libraries Unlimited, 1986. Also, *Full Speed Ahead, Glad Rags,* and *Raising the Roof.*

MacDonald, Margaret. *Book Sharing: 101 Programs to Use with Preschoolers.* Hamden, Conn.: Library Professional Publications, 1988.

Nespeca, Sue McCleaf. *Library Programming for Families with Young Children.* New York: Neal-Schuman, 1994.

Sitarz, Paula Gaj. *Picture Book Story Hours: From Birthdays to Bears.* Englewood, Colo.: Libraries Unlimited, 1987. Also, *More Picture Book Story Hours: From Parties to Pets.*

**General Activity Books To Expand
Literature for Preschool Story Programs**

Haas, Carolyn Buhai. *I Saw a Purple Cow.* Boston: Little, Brown, 1972. Also, *Purple Cow to the Rescue.*

Raines, Shirley, and Robert Canady. *Story Stretchers.* Mt. Rainier, Md.: Gryphon, 1989. Also, *More Story Stretchers.*

Warren, Jean. *Theme-A-Saurus.* Everett, Wash.: Warren, 1989. Also, *Theme-A-Saurus II* and *Storytime Theme-A-Saurus.*

Wilmes, Liz, and Dick Wilmes. *Circle Time.* Elgin, Ill.: Building Blocks, 1982. Also, *Everyday Circle Times, More Everyday Circle Times, Yearful of Circle Time,* etc.

Planning School-Age (K-3) Story Programs

Bauer, Caroline Feller. *Caroline Feller Bauer's New Handbook for Storytellers.* Chicago: American Library Association, 1993.

Bauer, Caroline Feller. *Celebrations.* New York: H.W. Wilson, 1985.

Bauer, Caroline Feller. *Handbook for Storytellers.* Chicago: American Library Association, 1977.

Bauer, Caroline Feller. *Read for the Fun of It.* New York: H.W. Wilson, 1991.

Bauer, Caroline Feller. *This Way to Books.* New York: H.W. Wilson, 1977.

Irving, Jan. *Fanfares: Programs for Classrooms & Libraries.* Englewood, Colo.: Libraries Unlimited, 1990.

MacDonald, Margaret Read. *Look Back and See: 20 Lively Tales for Gentle Tellers.* New York: H.W. Wilson, 1991.

MacDonald, Margaret Read. *Twenty Tellable Tales.* New York: H.W. Wilson, 1986.

MacDonald, Margaret Read. *When the Lights Go Out: 20 Scary Tales to Tell.* New York: H.W. Wilson,1988.

Pellowski, Anne. *Family Storytelling Handbook.* New York: Macmillan, 1987.

Pellowski, Anne. *The Story Vine: A Source Book of Unusual and Easy-to-Tell Stories From Around the World.* New York: Macmillan, 1984.

Peterson, Carolyn S. and Christina Sterchele. *Story Program Activities for Older Children.* Orlando, Fla.: Moonlight Press, 1987.

Raines, Shirley, and Robert Canady. *Story Stretchers for the Primary Grades.* Mt. Rainier, Md.: Gryphon, 1992.

Flannel/Magnetic/Velcro Board Stories and Pattern Books To Make Story Pieces

Briggs, Diane. *Flannel Board Fun: A Collection of Stories, Songs, and Poems.* Metuchen, N.J.: Scarecrow Press, 1992.

Forte, Imogene. *Kid's Stuff Book of Patterns, Projects and Plans.* Nashville, Tenn.: Incentive, 1982.

Kinghorn, Harriet, and Robert King. *Storytime Patterns for Eight Classic Children's Stories.* Minneapolis: T.S. Denison, 1990.

Sierra, Judy. *Flannelboard Storytelling Book.* New York: H.W. Wilson, 1987.

Sierra, Judy. *Multicultural Folktales: Stories to Tell Young Children.* Phoenix, Ariz.: Oryx, 1991.

Warren, Jean, comp. *Everyday Patterns.* Everett, Wash.: Warren, 1990. Also: *Animal Patterns, Holiday Patterns,* and *Nature Patterns.*

Wilmes, Liz, and Dick Wilmes. *Felt Board Fun.* Elgin, Ill.: Building Blocks, 1984.

Tell and Draw Stories and Cut and Tell Stories

Freedman, Barbara. *Draw Me a Story.* 4 Volumes. Fayetteville, N.C.: Feathered Nest Production, Inc., 1989.

Oldfield, Margaret Jean. *More Tell and Draw Stories*. Minneapolis: Creative Storytime Press, 1969. Also, *Lots More Tell and Draw Stories* and *Tell and Draw Stories* under author's last name of Olson, Margaret Jean.

Pflomm, Phyllis Noe. *Chalk In Hand: The Draw and Tell Book*. Metuchen, N.J.: Scarecrow Press, 1986.

Stangl, Jean. *Paper Stories*. Belmont, Calif.: Fearon, 1984.

Warren, Jean. *Cut and Tell: Scissor Stories for Fall*. Everett, Wash.: Warren, 1984. Also *Cut and Tell: Scissor Stories for Spring* and *Cut and Tell: Scissor Stories for Winter*.

Finger/Lap/Play/Action Rhymes and Songs

Beall, Pamela Conn, and Susan Hagen Nipp. *Wee Sing: Children's Songs and Fingerplays*. Los Angeles: Price/Stern/Sloan, 1981.

Brown, Marc, collector. *Finger Rhymes*. New York: Dutton, 1980. Also *Hand Rhymes, Party Rhymes,* and *Play Rhymes.*

Chorao, Kay. Baby's Lap Book. New York: Dutton, 1991.

Cole, Joanna, and Stephanie Calmenson, comps. *Eentsy, Weentsy Spider: Fingerplays and Action Rhymes*. New York: Morrow, 1991.

Cole, Joanna, and Stephanie Calmenson, comps. *Pat-A-Cake and Other Play Rhymes*. New York: Morrow, 1992.

Colgin, Mary Lou, comp. *One Potato, Two Potato, Three Potato, Four: 165 Chants for Children*. Mt. Rainier, Md: Gryphon, 1982.

Cromwell, Liz, Dixie Hibner, and John R. Faitel, comps. *Finger Frolics*. Rev. ed. Livonia, Mich.: Partner Press, 1983.

Defty, Jeff. *Creative Fingerplays and Action Rhymes*. Phoenix, Ariz.: Oryx, 1992.

Delamar, Gloria T. *Children's Counting-Out Rhymes, Fingerplays, Jump-Rope and Bounce-Ball Chants and Other Rhymes*. Jefferson, N.C.: McFarland, 1983.

Dowell, Ruth I. *Move Over, Mother Goose!* Mt. Rainier, Md.: Gryphon House, 1987.

Gawron, Marlene. *Busy Bodies: Finger Plays and Action Rhymes*. Orlando, Fla.: Moonlight Press, 1985.

Glazer, Tom. *Eye Winker, Tom Tinker, Chin Chopper: Fifty Musical Fingerplays*. New York: Doubleday, 1973.

Grayson, Marion F. *Let's Do Fingerplays*. Bridgeport: Robert B. Luce, 1962.

Hayes, Sarah, comp. *Clap Your Hands:Finger Rhymes*. New York: Lothrop, Lee & Shepard, 1988. Also, *Stamp Your Feet: Action Rhymes.*

McGee, Shelagh. *I'm a Little Teapot: Games Rhymes, and Songs for the First Three Years*. New York: Doubleday, 1990.

Matterson, Elizabeth. *Games for the Very Young*. New York: American Heritage Press, 1971.

Ra, Carol F. comp. *Trot Trot to Boston: Play Rhymes for Baby*. New York: Lothrop, Lee & Shepard, 1987.

Ring a Ring O'Roses. 9th ed. Flint, Mich.: Flint Public Library, 1988.

Roberts, Lynda. *Mitt Magic*. Mt. Rainier, MD.: Gryphon, 1985.

Scott, Louise Binder, and J.J. Thompson. *Rhymes for Fingers and Flannel Boards*. Minneapolis: T.S.Denison, 1984.

Williams, Sarah, collector. *Ride a Cock-Horse*. Oxford: Oxford University Press, 1986. Also, *Round and Round the Garden*.

Yolen, Jane, ed. The Lap-Time Song and Play Book. San Diego: Harcourt Brace, 1989.

Poetry/Nursery Rhyme Collections

De Paola, Tomie. *Tomie De Paola's Mother Goose*. New York: Putnam, 1985.

De Regniers, Beatrice Schenk, and others, selectors. *Sing a Song of Popcorn*. New York: Scholastic, 1988.

Emerson, Sally, selector. *Nursery Treasury: A Collection of Baby Games, Rhymes and Lullabies*. New York: Doubleday, 1988.

Foreman, Michael. *Michael Foreman's Mother Goose*. San Diego: Harcourt Brace, 1991.

Hopkins, Lee Bennett, collector. *Side by Side: Poems to Read Together*. New York: Simon & Schuster, 1988.

Kennedy, X.J., and Dorothy M. Kennedy. *Talking Like the Rain*. Boston: Little Brown, 1992.

Lobel, Arnold. *Random House Book of Mother Goose*. New York: Random, 1986.

Marks, Alan, selector. *Ring-a-Ring O' Roses and a Ding, Dong, Bell: A Collection of Nursery Rhymes*. Saxonville, Mass.: Picture Book Studio, 1991.

Mother Goose. *Wendy Watson's Mother Goose*. New York: Lothrop, Lee & Shepard, 1989.

Opie, Iona Archibald, and Peter Opie. *Tail Feathers From Mother Goose*. Boston: Little, Brown, 1988.

Prelutsky, Jack. *Beneath a Blue Umbrella*. New York: Greenwillow, 1990.

Prelutsky, Jack. *Read-Aloud Rhymes for the Very Young*. New York: Knopf, 1986.

Prelutsky, Jack. *Ride a Purple Pelican*. New York: Greenwillow, 1986.

Sutherland, Zena. *Orchard Book of Nursery Rhymes*. New York: Orchard, 1990.

Tortillitas Para Mama. New York: Holt, Rinehart and Winston, 1981.

Wright, Blanche. *Real Mother Goose*. New York: Macmillan, 1916.

Yolen, Jane. *The Three Bears Rhyme Book*. San Diego: Harcourt Brace, 1987.

Puppetry

Champlin, Connie. *Storytelling with Puppets*. Chicago: American Library Association, 1985.

Hunt, Tamara, and Nancy Renfro. *Pocketful of Puppets: Mother Goose*. Austin: Nancy Renfro Studios, 1982.

Hunt, Tamara, and Nancy Renfro. *Puppetry in Early Childhood Education*. Austin: Nancy Renfro Studios, 1979.

Shelton, Julie Catherine. *Puppets, Poems, and Songs*. Carthage, Ill.: Fearon, 1993.

Sierra, Judy. *Fantastic Theatre*. New York: H.W.Wilson, 1991.

Van Schuyver, Jan. *Storytelling Made Easy with Puppets*. Phoenix, Ariz.: Oryx, 1993.

Warren, Jean. *1-2-3 Puppets*. Everett, Wash.: Warren, 1989.

Williams, DeAtna M. *Paper-Bag Puppets.* Carthage, Ill.: Fearon, 1966. Also, *More Paper-Bag Puppets.*

Wright, Denise Anton. *One-Person Puppet Plays.* Englewood, Colo.: Libraries Unlimited, 1990.

Song Books

Barrett, Carol. *Mother Goose Songbook.* New York: Derrydale Books, 1986.

Beall, Pamela Conn, and Nipp, Susan Hagen. *Wee Sing* series. Los Angeles: Price/Stern/Sloan.

Browne, Jane. *Sing Me a Story.* New York: Crown, 1991.

Emerson, Sally, comp. *The Kingfisher Nursery Rhyme Songbook.* New York: Kingfisher, 1992.

Glazer, Tom. *Music for Ones and Twos: Songs and Games for the Very Young Child.* New York: Doubleday, 1983. Also *The Mother Goose Songbook, Do Your Ears Hang Low,* and *Eye Winker, Tom Tinker, Chin Chopper* (also listed above under finger rhymes).

Hart, Jane, comp. *Singing Bee!* New York: Lothrop, Lee & Shepard, 1982.

Larrick, Nancy, comp. *Songs From Mother Goose.* New York: HarperCollins, 1989.

Mattox, Cheryl Warren, collector. *Shake it to the One That You Love the Best.* El Sobrante, Calif.: Warren-Mattox Productions, 1989.

Nelson, Esther. *Everybody Sing and Dance.* Cleveland, Ohio.: Instructor Books, 1989.

Palmer, Hap. *Baby Songs.* New York: Crown, 1990.

Raffi. *Raffi Singable Songbook.* New York: Crown, 1987. Also, *2nd Raffi Songbook.*

Schiller, Pam and Thomas Moore. *Where is Thumbkin?* Mt. Rainier, Md.: Gryphon, 1993.

Sharon, Lois & Bram. *Elephant Jam.* New York: Crown, 1989. Also *Sharon, Lois & Bram's Mother Goose,* and *Sharon, Lois & Bram Sing A to Z.*

Warren, Jean. *Piggyback Songs.* Everett, Wash.: Warren, 1983. Also *Animal Piggyback Songs, Holiday Piggyback Songs, More Piggyback Songs, Piggyback Songs For Infants and Toddlers,* and *Piggyback Songs to Sign.*

Weiss, Nicki. *If You're Happy and You Know It: Eighteen Story Songs Set to Pictures.* New York: Greenwillow, 1987.

Weissman, Jackie. *My Toes Are Starting to Wiggle.* Overland Park, Kan.: Miss Jackie Music Company, 1991.

Weissman, Jackie. *Songs to Sing with Babies.* Mt. Rainier, Md.: Gryphon, 1983.

Wirth, Marion. *Musical Games, Fingerplays, Rhythmic Activities for Early Childhood.* West Nyack, N.Y.: Parker Publishing, 1985.

Yolen, Jane, ed. *Jane Yolen's Mother Goose Songbook.* Honesdale, Pa.: Boyds Mill Press, 1992.

Art Activities

Bos, Bev. *Don't Move the Muffin Tins: A Hands-Off Guide to Art for the Young Child.* Roseville, Calif.: Turn-The-Page Press, Inc., 1978.

Brashears, Deya. *Dribble Drabble: Art Experiences for Young Children.* Mt. Rainier, Md.: Gryphon, 1985.

Brashears, Deya, and Lea Brashears. *More. . .Dribble Drabble.* Orinda, Calif.: Circle Time Publishing, 1992.

Kohl, Mary. *Scribble Cookies.* Bellingham, WA.: Bright Ring, 1985. Also, *Mudworks.*

True, Susan. *Nursery Rhyme Crafts.* Palo Alto, Calif.: Monday Morning Books, 1985.

Warren, Jean, compiler. *1-2-3 Art.* Everett, Wash.: Warren, 1985.

Wilmes, Liz, and Dick Wilmes. *Exploring Art.* Elgin, Ill.: Building Blocks, 1986.

Wilmes, Liz, and Dick Wilmes. *Paint Without Brushes.* Elgin, Ill.: Building Blocks, 1993.

ENDNOTES

1. Ann D. Carlson, *The Preschooler and the Library.* (Metuchen, N.J.: Scarecrow Press, 1991), p. 16.

2. Ibid., p. 17.

3. Ibid., p. 19.

4. Ibid., p. 22.

5. Jerry West and Elvie Germino Hausken, *Profile of Preschool Children's Child Care and Early Education Program Participation.* (Washington, D.C.: U.S. Department of Education Office of Educational Research and Improvement, 1993), p. 7.

6. Helen Cannon and Joyce Dixon, "Parents, New Babies, and Books," *School Library Journal* (January 1988): 68.

5 PROGRAMS FOR THE ENTIRE FAMILY

Often libraries will offer programs that the entire family can attend together, even if children are of varying ages. Though programs will not be as developmentally appropriate in these instances, there are advantages to having a program that the whole family can enjoy together.

There are several reasons libraries may want to offer these mixed-age-group programs:

1. Libraries are small and have limited space for programs.
2. Library resources (money and/or staff) are in short supply. All programming results in costs to the library: money, time, and number of staff needed. If there is only one staff member serving children, or only one person responsible for all library programming, having several different story-time programs may be impossible. Libraries often operate with limited resources and simply cannot afford to have infant, toddler, preschool, and school-age story programs along with family-literacy, multicultural, and intergenerational programs. They feel that their time is best spent offering programs to the entire family at one time.
3. Some libraries may have staff and time, but merely want to involve the entire family unit in a program so that families can appreciate reading and books simultaneously.

Though this type of programming relies less on the developmental stages of young children in planning, these stages still must be kept in mind when planning. Librarians also might want to provide bookmarks or reading lists to caregivers attending these programs, listing appropriate materials and activities for various developmental/age levels. Caregivers then will have an idea of what books to choose and how to share literacy activities with their young children. Another excellent handout would list several recommended anthologies that can be enjoyed by families with children of various ages. (See Fig. 3.2 in Chapter 3 for suggestions of anthologies that would be appropriate reading for young children of varying ages.)

For books that will be helpful when planning family storytime programs, see the section "Planning School-Age (K-3) Story Programs" in the bibliography "Resources for Librarians Who Serve Young Children" in Chapter 4 (see Page 104). Another excellent resource in *Library Service for Families* by Marguerite Baechtold and Eleanor Ruth McKinney (Library Professional Publications, 1983).

Following are 20 sample programs that can be done with the entire family. Three in particular will be featured at the end of this chapter (see Fig. 5.1; 5.2; 5.3). They include a family storytime presentation; a family project of making books together; and a family reading program, called Book Bingo. Also, family-history, multicultural, and intergenerational programs that are suitable for families with children of varying ages will be highlighted in Chapter 6.

Sample Program: Make-It Take-It Puppetry

Families can make easy puppets to be used in shows at the library and/or that can be taken home for family puppet shows. Librarians can demonstrate several types of puppets made out of household items such as small paper bags, large grocery bags, paper plates, empty tubes, envelopes, spoons, egg cartons, socks, mitts, etc. You need space for families to work and numerous supplies, though families can provide some of their own items such as grocery bags, egg cartons, socks, etc. This program can be expanded to cover several weeks. The first week, a puppet show can be held for the families. The second week, a make-it take-it session with librarians, providing simple puppet scripts for the families to practice, could follow. At a third meeting, families could use their puppets to present shows for the other families or children. Puppet books with easy puppets to make for families with young children include *Pocketful of Puppets: Mother Goose* and *Puppetry in Early Childhood Education,* both by Tamara Hunt and Nancy Renfro from Nancy Renfro Studios. Also *1-2-3 Puppets* by Jean Warren (Warren Press) and *Puppets, Poems, and Songs* by Julie Catherine Shelton (Fearon Press) contain easy-to-make puppets requiring basic supplies. For simple scripts, consult *One-Person Puppet Plays* by Denise Wright from Libraries Unlimited (the plays can be performed by one or several people), *Storytelling Made Easy With Puppets* by Jan Van Schuyver (Oryx), and Judy Sierra's *Fantastic Theater* (H.W. Wilson).

Sample Program: Art Fun for Families

Families can create art projects together and display the results in the library. Demonstrate some open-ended art projects and let families try using various mediums. Provide some "recipes" so families can enjoy producing their own art at home. This program also lends itself well to a two-week session. After demonstrating and letting families explore the first week, have them plan a special art project they would like to do together the second week. They can then exhibit their creation for a special month-long "art show." Consult some excellent open-ended art project books, such as *Dribble Drabble: Art Experiences for Young Children* and *More . . . Dribble Drabble,* both by Deya Brashears; *Scribble Cookies* and *Mudworks* by Mary Kohl; *Exploring Art and Paint Without Brushes* by Liz and Dick Wilmes; and *1-2-3 Art* by Jean Warren. Another way to enjoy different types of art is by sharing some books with unusual or striking picture-book art such as those by Lois Ehlert, Denise Fleming, or Eric Carle, and demonstrate ways to "mimic" the type of art in these illustrations. Have families try making collages, etc.

Sample Program: Rhyme & Rap

Often even families that read aloud regularly rarely share books of poetry with their young children. Many picture books are written in rhyme; these can be shared with families in a family program, but it is also a great idea to share some of the wonderful poetry books there are for young children, such as Lee Bennett Hopkins' *Side by Side*; Jack Prelutsky's *Read-Aloud Rhymes for the Very Young* or *Ride a Purple Pelican*; or X. J. Kennedy's *Talking Like the Rain*. Several books by professional storyteller Carolyn Feller Bauer are helpful in making poetry fun for children and families with props, poetry trees, etc. Families can clap along or snap their fingers with the beat of stories such as *Chicka Chicka Boom Boom* by Bill Martin and John Archambault, or *Crocodile Beat* by Gail Jorgensen. Families also can make their own homemade poetry books with some of their favorite poems, and children can illustrate these books.

Sample Program: Exploring the World of Science

There are several elementary science project books that make science fun for the whole family (rather than school-project-oriented guides). Librarians can demonstrate several entertaining projects or science mysteries and have families investigate some of their own. Choose not only easy projects but ones that young children can help with in some manner. Check science-experiment books by Vicki Cobb, *The Science Book of Numbers* by Jack Challoner, or *My First Science Book* by Angela Wilkes. Another suggestion is to share an easy science-concept book from the wonderful *Eye Openers* series (Aladdin Books, first published by Dorling Kindersley in Great Britain), such as *Planes*. After sharing this nonfiction book on planes (include some picture books if you wish), talk about planes and have families make paper airplanes.

Sample Program: Exploring Space

Do you have a planetarium in your community? Is there an astronomer at a local college who would be willing to talk to young children and their families about space? Can you borrow a small telescope that families can try out? Display star charts and talk about constellations. Even young children can help make star charts. Use blue paper and white shoe polish. Share the book *Stargazer* by Gail Gibbons. What would it be like to travel in space? Have families convey their views. What would they want to take with them? What do astronauts eat? Read the book *The Magic School Bus Lost in the Solar System* by Joanna Cole, and picture books such as *A Trip to Mars* by Ruth Young and *Dogs in Space* by Nancy Coffelt.

Sample Program: Exploring the Ocean

What lives in the sea? Talk about fish, whales, dolphins, sharks, sea urchins, sea horses, anemones, mussels, lobsters, crabs, scorpions, seaweed, tide pools, etc. Share the book *The Magic School Bus on the Ocean Floor* by Joanna Cole and several picture books such as *What if the Shark Wears Tennis Shoes, Hermit the Crab* by Eric Carle, and *Going on a Whale Watch* by Bruce McMillan. Folkmanis Puppets in Emeryville, Calif., has several sea-creature puppets that would enliven a program on the ocean. And at the end of any program on the ocean, you must share goldfish crackers.

The last several programs mentioned above explored science concepts, space and the ocean. You could hold a series of "Let's Explore" family programs on a weekly or monthly basis. Other suggestions for areas to explore include nature and the environment.

Sample Program: Fun With Numbers

There are many simple but fun number games that families can play together. Check any game book for ideas. Magic books also have simple tricks that involve numbers or items to be counted. Keep the numbers low so children can help add, etc. There are also card number games such as Flinch. Bruce McMillan's book *Eating Fractions* may give you ideas of ways food can be cut up to make fractions. Books with number concepts that could be shared include such titles as: *Only One* by Marc Harshman, *How Many, How Many, How Many* by Rick Walton, *Counting Sheep to Sleep* by Mary O'Brien, *One Hundred Hungry Ants* by Elinor Pinczes, *12 Ways to Get to 11* by Eve Merriam, *Mother Earth's Counting Book* by Andrew Clements, and, for one-on-one sharing, *From One to One Hundred* by Teri Sloat.

Sample Program: Music, Music Everywhere!

There is an endless amount of ideas for a music program for families. Sing-alongs are popular, particularly if you select favorite songs from childhood or camp tunes. There are probably folk singers in your area that would be willing to perform or others talented in playing unusual instruments, such as dulcimers, accordions, or banjos. You can provide instruments for families to play along with recordings. For basic rhythm-band instruments, an excellent ordering source is Rhythm Band Instruments, P.O. Box 126, Fort Worth, TX 76101; 1-800-424-4724. If you can afford some multicultural instruments, Lakeshore Learning Materials (2695 E. Dominguez St., Carson, CA 90749; 1-800-421-5354) has a set of ten multicultural instruments that you can use after telling folk tales from other countries. Provide families with a bibliography of recommended CDs and cassettes, and play some recordings, asking the families to sing or clap along with the music.

Another project for families to work on together is making simple musical instruments. Consult such sources as: Hap Palmer's *Homemade Band; My First Music Book* by Helen Drew; and *Shake, Tap, and Play a Merry Tune* by Tania Cowling (Fearon). Make sure you make a display of song books (see the Chapter Four section on "Song Books" under the bibliography "Resources for Librarians Who Serve Young Children" see Page 107) and share several song picture books. Some favorites for young children include: *I Know an Old Lady Who Swallowed a Fly* by Glen Rounds, *Skip to My Lou* by Nadine Bernard Westcott, *In a Cabin in a Wood* adapted by Darcie McNally, *The Itsy Bitsy Spider* by Iza Trapani, and numerous picture-book versions of Raffi songs such as "Down by the Bay" and "Spider on the Floor."

Sample Program: Family Picnic and Games

A family picnic with old-fashioned picnic games, party games, or some of the non-competitive games featured in outdoor-game books allow families to mix with each other but also be together as a family. (Consult books such as Joanna Cole and Stephanie Calmenson's *Pin the Tail on the Donkey and Other Party Games, Everybody Wins: 393 Non-Competitive Games for Young Children* by Jeffrey Sobel, and *The Second Cooperative Sports and Games Book* by Terry Orlick.) Tell some stories around a fake campfire (Margaret MacDonald's storytelling books have some great tales), have families enjoy their own picnic lunches, then play games. Volunteers may want to make "coffee can" ice cream and let children make their own sundaes. Indoor games and a picnic is also a possibility and should be planned in case of rain!

Sample Program: Toys, Toys, Toys

Families can benefit from a discussion of what toys are not only educational, but also safe. The U.S. Consumer Product Safety Commission in Washington, D.C., publishes a brochure and posters yearly concerning toys that are safe. There are also guides to toys that are developmentally appropriate for children at different stages. Toy stores may set up a display of safe and educational toys and puzzles for families to see. A teacher in early childhood education would be able to speak on the topic of appropriate toys for certain ages. You can also have a make-it take-it session of some simple toys that families can make.

Sample Program: Good Videos for Children

Children often spend as much time watching videos as they do television. Families need to be cautioned on the amount of time children sit in front of a television set watching programs or videos. They can often also use guidance on what videos are good for their children if a limited amount of time is devoted to video watching weekly. Librarians can talk about how to evaluate videos and can show several videos as examples. Some resource guides that might be helpful are: *Preschool Resource Guide: Educating and Entertaining Children Aged Two Through Five* by Harriet Friedes and *Great Videos for Kids: A Parent's Guide to Choosing The Best* (Citadel Press, 600 Madison Ave., 11th Fl., New York, NY 10022). The videocassette *Choosing the Best in Children's Videos* by the American Library Association (1990) also can be shown.

Sample Program: Plants and Gardening

An ideal late-spring family program is one on planting flowers and vegetable gardens. Even the youngest of children can help plant. Families do not even need to have property to plant such things as tomatoes or flowers in pots. Families can be given seeds to start in paper cups at the library. Good resource books are *My First Garden Book* by Angela Wilkes, *How a Seed Grows* by Helene Jordan, and *The Reason for a Flower* by Ruth Heller. There are many picture-book stories to share on plants and gardens, such as Lois Ehlert's *Planting a Rainbow* or *Growing Vegetable Soup,* Paul Galdone's *Little Red Hen, Jasper's Beanstalk* by Nick Butterworth and Mick Inkpen, *A Garden Alphabet* by Isabel Wilner, and *The Carrot Seed* by Ruth Krauss. Children also can make seed and grain pictures.

Sample Program: Dinosaur Dig

Young children are fascinated with dinosaurs. Families can go on a dinosaur dig together, discovering different types of dinosaurs, singing dinosaur songs, watching a dinosaur film, playing dinosaur games, and making dinosaur art prints (paint with dinosaur cookie cutters). Discuss what dinosaurs ate, how they differed, and what caused them to disappear. Dinosaur books to share are plentiful but some of the best nonfiction books for young children are by Aliki and Byron Barton. Scholastic's *First Discovery Book of Dinosaurs* and Jan Pienkowski's pop-up book *ABC Dinosaurs and Other Prehistoric Creatures* will fascinate young children. Different shape dinosaur cookies to eat make a perfect ending for a dinosaur dig party.

Sample Program: Let's Go to the Circus!

This is the perfect family program to hold at your library about two weeks before the circus comes to town. Not only can you share circus stories, talk about what families will see at the circus, and hold mini-circus acts, but you can also have a clown or juggler perform. Add some face painting, circus or animal songs, and popcorn, and you have an ideal program that will prepare families for the circus experience. Because you will be giving the circus publicity, you might see if you can get some free tickets for prizes.

Sample Program: Petting Zoo

A popular family activity is a petting zoo. Though it may take some arranging, it is usually not too difficult to find someone who will bring a few farm pets or a park naturalist who will bring some snakes to (or outside of!) the library. Have the presenter tell about the animals' habits, food, care, and the like. Share some stories about pets or animals, and tell families ahead of time to bring along their favorite stuffed pet. You may wish to make some patterns similar to the ones found in Lois Ehlert's unusual shape books *Color Farm* and *Color Zoo* and have the children take the shape patterns and design their own animals/pets.

Sample Program: Sign Language

Even preschool children can learn sign language, and most families will have an interest in learning sign language whether or not they use it on a regular basis. Tell some folk tales or stories that have repeating words that can be signed, and teach family members the signs for those words. The family will have the opportunity to make the signs every time you use those words. Simple songs

FIGURE 5.1 Family Night at the Library—TV Newscast Based on Children's Literature

Contact Persons: Mary Anne Russo and Nancy Grapevine

Library: Hubbard Public Library, Hubbard, Ohio

Brief Description: This library holds a series of Family Nights, begun in response to patrons who asked why programs had to be limited to certain age groups. The solution was doing programs for the entire family, with the added benefit of providing an evening of free quality time which families could share. This particular program was done with the help of a guest storyteller, a popular local sportscaster from a local TV channel. Other parts in the newscast were performed by librarians or staff members.

Script: Prime Time

Anchor Person (Youth Services Librarian): Good evening, and welcome to Channel READ News. Our top story tonight involves a case of breaking and entering at the home of the Three Bears. For the complete story, let's go to our reporter on the scene in the forest, (Name of Staff Member).

Reporter (Staff Member): Tells the story of *Goldilocks and the Three Bears*.

Anchor Person (Youth Services Librarian): Thank you, (Name of Reporter).
(For the rest of the "news stories" below, book covers were projected onto a wall with an opaque projector.) In other news tonight, tragedy was averted when a wolf tried to pass himself off as Little Red Riding Hood's grandmother. Fortunately, Little Red was rescued by a passing woodsman. The wolf was held for questioning by local police.

Good news tonight in the case of Spot, the yellow puppy who was reported missing by his mother, Sally. As Sally asked, "*Where's Spot?*", volunteers searched in the closet, under the stairs, and numerous other places until Spot was finally located in a basket. He was returned to his mother just in time for supper.

An unidentified flying object was seen over the area today. Witnesses reported a large goose-like creature being ridden by an elderly woman. Authorities are investigating.

A disturbance was reported today at the home of two area children. The youngsters were visited by a cat wearing a red and white striped hat. Although the family goldfish reported that the cat made a mess of the place, no injures were reported.

We'll be back after these words from our sponsor.

Takeoffs on two popular commercials (performed by librarians and staff members):

First Alert—"I'm reading and I don't want to get up."

American Express—"Your Library Card—Don't leave home without it."

Anchor Person (Youth Services Librarian): And now, for the latest news in the world of sports, featuring a report on today's big race between *The Tortoise and the Hare,* here's (Name of Local Sportscaster).

Local TV Sportscaster: Reads *The Tortoise and the Hare.*

Anchor Person (Youth Services Librarian):Thanks, (Name of Local Sportscaster). With a look at our weather forecast, here's our own, (Name of Youth Services Staff Member).

Weather Reporter (Youth Services Staff Member): Tells story, *Cloudy With a Chance of Meatballs.*

Anchor Person (Youth Services Librarian):Thanks, (Name of Youth Services Staff Member). It sounds as though we're in for a delicious day. That concludes our news for tonight. Stay tuned to your Library and Channel READ for many more exciting upcoming events. Good night, and good reading.

FIGURE 5.2 Family Book-Making Project

One very fun project that the entire family can enjoy together is making books. In Chapter 6, there are several examples of family history books to make. Here the emphasis is on books with unique moveable parts. Most young children are fascinated by books with intriguing design. Flap books, pop-up books, and other manipulative books are developmentally appropriate for very young children who have a natural curiosity and like to learn by touching. Slightly older children also seem to like the unusual action quality of such books.

Librarians can demonstrate several types of books to make such as pop-up, accordion, shape, tab, or wheel books. Families can then make up a story together and decide on a design of their choice. This can be a project that can take place over two weeks. Librarians can first share some story books with unique design and then demonstrate the processes of making such books. Families can create their own story together during the following week and come back to the library to make their books with librarian encouragement or assistance. Books can be displayed for others to read.

Librarians can furnish materials to make books or have families provide their own supplies. Supplies can be as simple as construction paper, typing or computer paper, glue sticks, scissors, crayons, and markers. Pages can be stapled together or hole punched and tied with ribbon or string. Make sure the family includes an author page with a picture of the family and a brief family history!

Several resources that will be helpful for families making books or that can be used by librarians to demonstrate how to make uniquely designed books follow.

Resource Books Useful for Making Books with Young Children

Evans, Joy, and Jo Ellen Moore. *How to Make Books With Children.* Monterey, Calif.: Evan-Moor, 1984.

Evans, Joy, Kathleen Morgan, and Jo Ellen Moore. *Making Big Books with Children.* Monterey, Calif.: Evan-Moor, 1989.

Irvine, Joan. *How to Make Super Pop-Ups.* New York: Beech Tree Books, 1992.

Johnson, Paul. *A Book of One's Own: Developing Literacy Through Making Books.* Portsmouth, N.H.: Heinemann, 1990.

Ketch, Susan. *Making Books for Winter.* Greensboro, N.C.: Carson-Dellosa Publishing, 1992.

Ketch, Susan, *Making Books for Fall.* Greensboro, N.C.: Carson-Dellosa Publishing, 1992.

Ling, Patricia. *Making Books for Spring and Summer.* Greensboro, N.C.: Carson-Dellosa Publishing, 1992.

Pellowski, Anne. *How To Make Cloth Books: A Guide to Making Personalized Books.* Radnor, Pa.: Chilton Book Company, 1992.

FIGURE 5.3 Family Funtime Book Bingo

Contact Person: Carol Carmack

Library: Stark County District Library, Canton, Ohio

Brief Description: Book bingo was established to encourage families to spend time together reading for enjoyment and knowledge.

"Welcome to Family Funtime Book Bingo, sponsored by the Stark County District Library and Papa Bear's Pizza. If you complete two bingos by January 16, you will receive a free ticket to a presentation of *Jack and the Beanstalk* performed by the Haga Hayes Marionette Puppeteers on January 23 at the Main Library. Show times are 1:00 and 3:00 P.M. Good luck and good reading!"

Family Funtime Book Bingo Rules

1. All family members (all ages) are encouraged to participate, with adults and children reading to each other.
2. You must complete two rows of bingo to receive your free ticket to the puppet show. Bingos can be vertical, horizontal, or diagonal.
3. Color each square when it is completed.
4. Write the author/title of the book you read on the corresponding number line (on back of the card).
5. Start now and be sure to turn in your card no later than January 16.

Participating family members (list names here).
We have completed Family Funtime Book Bingo: (Date)
Signature of Head of Family.

1 Multi–Cultural	2 Cook Something From a Book	3 Bedtime Story	4 Non-Fiction	5 Folk and Fairy Tales
6 Science or Space	7 Favorite Author	8 The Arts	9 Poetry	10 Fiction
11 Weekend Storytime	12 Classic	13 Family Story	14 Biography	15 Listen to a Book–on–Tape
16 Folk and Fairy Tales	17 Magazine	18 Dinosaur Story	19 Visit to the Library	20 Country, State, or Travel Book
21 Make Something From a Book	22 Mystery	23 Animal	24 Family Story	25 Holiday Story

requiring just a few signs also can be taught. You might want to prepare some basic handouts so family members have something to take home to practice and remember.

Sample Program: New Families in the Community

A wonderful outreach program is to attempt to reach new families that have moved to your community. If there is a Welcome Wagon organization, you should be able to find out who these families are, but public schools also might be able to give you names of children who have moved to the area. Invite these new families to the library, explaining your services and programs. Have a family storytime program and provide booklists and bookmarks. Family members can sign up for library cards if they do not already have them. If funds permit, give away a paperback book to each family. Not only might you make some new library patrons, but it is a wonderful way for families to meet others new to the community. You also might want to have representatives of other service organizations available to explain their services.

6 FAMILY-HISTORY, MULTICULTURAL, AND INTERGENERATIONAL PROGRAMS

There is probably no library program that can draw a family closer together than one that encourages families to discover and explore their history or share some of their family stories. These programs can involve oral family storytelling and also writing the stories in a book or journal, accompanied by children's illustrations and/or photographs. As mentioned in Chapter 1, families can be defined in various ways. Children may be adopted, or be part of a "blended" family, or have two parents of the same sex, or have a grandparent as their caregiver. There is still family history to research, write, and share. There are many types of programs that libraries can offer in which families will feel like a special unit that belongs together and has special memories to share. And what better place than a library to execute such programs? Not only are there many books on searching family roots, there are books on how to tape oral biographies, numerous ideas on how to make books, and resource books that encourage family-history sharing. Librarians can suggest each family make its own individual family-history book, or one book can be made for the library containing different family vignettes. Numerous suggestions for different types of family-history explorations and programming follow.

Family Favorites: Have each family share some of their favorite things. They can make a poster with their family picture, then list some of their favorite things, such as favorite food, movie, place to visit, game, TV show, and book (of course!). Photos or pictures cut from magazines of some of the family favorites can be included on the poster. Then have each family share its favorites and briefly tell about them to others in the group.

Taping Family Life Stories: Families can audiotape or videotape (with library equipment) their life stories. Children can ask questions of family members to find out what it was like for them growing up. Where were they born? Where did they live? What was school like? Where was their favorite place to visit? Who were their friends? An excellent resource helpful for audiotaping or videotaping family life stories is *How to Tape Instant Oral Biographies* by Bill Zimmerman.[1]

Making Family Calendars: This is a good program for the end of the year. Have monthly calendar pages for the next year stapled together for each family. Leave the top part of the page of each month blank. Have families draw pictures for each month of family activities that they enjoy that month, or use family photos on each month's page. Have the families make the calendars together and mark important dates for their family on their calendar.

Family Vacation Journals: Families going on vacation or on a "special day out" can record their day's activity or vacation in a journal. Photos or illustrations can be included. Have them share with other families.

Family Picnic: Have a family picnic with each family bringing one of their favorite foods to share. Play games that involve the whole family as a unit, but which require cooperation among family members. Make sure they are noncompetitive games so that families are not really competing against each other, but rather must work together to complete a goal. Families can cheer other families on!

My Family's Favorite Person: Have each family bring along a person who is special to them to your program. Have them tell who this special person is and why they are special to the family. It could be a grandparent, aunt, uncle, neighbor, teacher, or family friend.

Family Holidays: Have each family share how they celebrate a certain holiday or their favorite holiday. They can mention their various traditions and bring along items to show that go along with the holiday.

Family-History Books: Have each family make a family-history book. The first page can be a simplified family tree. Stories about family history can follow, along with photos or children's drawings.

Family Puppets: Have family members make puppets out of materials you provide. (They can be spoon puppets, glove puppets, paper-plate puppets, paper-bag puppets etc.) Each member will make a puppet resembling himself or herself. Then have each family go to a puppet stage and "present" their family. If you do not have a puppet stage, drape a black dropcloth, tablecloth, or other large piece of material over a table and have family members sit on the floor or on small stools or chairs behind the table. They can each introduce themselves with their puppet and tell something about themselves (such as their age, hobbies, etc.)

My Life: Have each child in the family make a journal of their life up to that point. They should do it year by year. For example, they can list on one page "Where I was born" and include photos or information supplied to them by the caregiver. The next page would be "Age One." A photo or drawing can be placed on top of the page with something special that occurred that year. Again, information can be supplied by the child or caregiver.

Meet My Family: Have each family make a book where they answer the same questions. Illustrate or include photos. Questions can include how many people are in the family and who they are, the favorite family activity is . . . , the family has the following pets, the family's favorite food is . . . , etc. Have one family member from each family share the book with the rest of the families.

Make a Family Tree: Have a twig with several branches for each child. Secure them in a coffee can or planting pot with soil. Have each child hang a photo (or drawn picture) of each family member from the branches. If you cannot have a twig for each child, have a stick or ruler in each pot and have the children attach pictures or drawings to them. Each child can then introduce their family at the program.

Family Storytimes: Share stories that emphasize families or family life. Then have families share an interesting story about their family. Picture books and easy fiction stories that are good for sharing and depict family life are listed next (see Fig. 6.1).

Fascinating Family Folklore: Make up a book for your library of family folklore from various families. Reproduce the book and distribute it to all families that contributed. One library successfully accomplished this during their summer reading program. Their program follows (see Fig. 6.2).

FIGURE 6.1 Books for Family Storytimes That Depict Family Life

---

In addition to the books listed here, consider the lists of multicultural family stories and intergenerational stories in this chapter that are also excellent for family storytimes.

Bartone, Elisa. *Peppe the Lamplighter*. New York: Lothrop, Lee & Shepard, 1993.

> Peppe is a member of an Italian family new to America at the turn-of-the-century in New York. His dream is to become a lamplighter, though this is not what his father has planned for him.

Cooper, Melrose. *I Got a Family*. New York: Henry Holt, 1993.

> A young girl describes her family—a Great-Gran; a Grampy; an Uncle; an Auntie; a brother; a Daddy; a Mamma; and a kitty—and how she loves them, and they love her.

Crews, Donald. *Bigmama's*. New York: Greenwillow, 1991.

> The author describes what it was like visiting his Grandma in the summertime in Florida. Cousins, friends, and family were all there to talk to and have fun with during the long, hot months.

Crews, Donald. *Short Cut*. New York: Greenwillow, 1992.

> The children decide to take a shortcut home by walking on the railroad tracks near Bigmama's house and almost get hit by a train.

Dragonwagon, Crescent. *Home Place*. New York: Macmillan, 1990.

> A family goes out hiking and discovers certain relics from long ago, making them wonder about the family that originally lived there.

Flournoy, Valerie. *Patchwork Quilt*. New York: Dial, 1985.

> Grandma begins making a quilt from scraps of material left from family members' clothing to tell the story of the family's life. When she gets ill, Tanya and her Mom finish it, to fulfill a family tradition.

Friedman, Ina R. *How My Parents Learned To Eat*. Boston: Houghton Mifflin, 1984.

> A young girl tells the story of why on some days they eat with chopsticks and other days with a knife and fork. The amusing story tells of the courtship of her Japanese mother and American father.

Greenwald, Sheila. *Rosy Cole Discovers America!* Boston: Little, Brown, 1992.

> Rosy's teacher has her class discover America by searching their family history and sharing it with the class. At first, Rosy makes up stories to make her family sound more interesting, until she realizes her family history is exciting in itself!

Grifalconi, Ann. *Kinda Blue*. Boston: Little, Brown, 1993.

> Sissy is feeling kind of blue when she thinks her whole family is ignoring her until Uncle Dan shows her how even corn needs special love and attention.

Heath, Amy. *Sofie's Role*. New York: Four Winds, 1992.

> On the day before Christmas, Sofie gets to help her family serving customers behind the counter in their bakery business.

FIGURE 6.1 Continued

Hoffman, Mary. *Amazing Grace.* New York: Dial, 1991.

Grace, who loves stories, decides she wants to be Peter Pan in the class play. Though other children in her class say she can not be since she is a girl and black, Ma and Nana show her she can be anything she wants to be.

Hopkinson, Deborah. *Sweet Clara and the Freedom Quilt.* New York: Knopf, 1993.

Clara, who is separated from her mother at age 11 and sent to a different plantation, becomes a seamstress in the owner's house. Carefully, over a period of months, she collects information on how to escape to the underground railroad, and hides the map in a quilt. She escapes to freedom along with her mother and new little sister.

Houston, Gloria. *My Great-Aunt Arizona.* New York: HarperCollins, 1992.

The author relates the story of her Great-Aunt Arizona who was born in a log cabin in the Blue Ridge Mountains and who loved to read and dream of the faraway places she wanted to visit. Though she never got to travel, she became a teacher and taught children about those faraway places.

Howard, Elizabeth. *Aunt Flossie's Hats (And Crab Cakes Later.)* New York: Clarion, 1991.

Sarah and Susan visit their favorite relative, Great-Great-Aunt Flossie, every Sunday afternoon and hear stories from her past.

Hudson, Wade. *I Love My Family.* New York: Scholastic, 1993.

A young boy describes a family reunion and how much fun he has.

Johnson, Angela. *The Girl Who Wore Snakes.* New York: Orchard, 1993.

Ali loves snakes, though no one else around her does. She wonders why she is so different, until she meets one of her aunts.

Johnson, Angela. *One of Three.* New York: Orchard, 1991.

A young girl states what it is like to be one of three sisters, and also special times, when it is just her, Mama, and Daddy together.

Johnson, Angela. *Tell Me a Story,* Mama. New York: Orchard, 1989.

At bedtime, a young girl asks her Mom to recall stories from childhood.

Mitchell, Barbara. *Down Buttermilk Lane.* New York: Lothrop, Lee & Shepard, 1993.

An Amish family from Lancaster, PA, travel by buggy to the village to do some errands.

Mitchell, Margaree King. *Uncle Jed's Barbershop.* New York: Simon & Schuster, 1993.

Sarah Jean's Uncle Jed was a black barber in the segregated South during the 1920s who had to travel around the countryside to cut hair. His dream to own his own barber shop is realized right before his death.

Patrick, Denise Lewis. *Car Washing Street.* New York: Tambourine, 1993.

Matthew looks forward to Saturday mornings when everyone in the neighborhood washes family cars, and his whole family joins in, having a wonderful time.

FIGURE 6.1 Continued

Pellegrini, Nina. *Families are Different*. New York: Holiday, 1991.

Nico and her sister Angel, from Korea, are adopted by an American family. Nico realizes that all families are different.

Pinkney, Gloria Jean. *Back Home*. New York: Dial, 1992.

Eight-year-old Ernestine, who lives in a city up north, visits Uncle June, Aunt Beula, and Cousin Jack at the family farm in North Carolina where she was born and where her Mama grew up.

Pringle, Laurence. *Octopus Hug*. Honesdale, Pa.: Boyds Mills Press, 1993.

Mom goes out for the evening with a friend and Dad gets to entertain the children with all kinds of games and fun, such as octopus hugs.

Rattigan, Jama Kim. *Dumpling Soup*. Boston: Little, Brown, 1993.

Marisa gets to help make dumplings for the first time for Grandma's soup that is eaten at midnight at the family's annual gathering to celebrate New Year's Eve on the Hawaiian islands.

Rylant, Cynthia. *The Relatives Came*. New York: Bradbury, 1985.

The author describes an amusing view of her family life, when her relatives from Virginia come to visit and "stay and stay."

Rylant, Cynthia. *When I Was Young in the Mountains*. New York: Dutton, 1981.

The author shares how it was growing up with her family in Appalachia.

Shelby, Anne. *We Keep a Store*. New York: Orchard, 1990.

A young girl explains what it is like to help her family run its country store.

Tate, Eleanora E. *Front Porch Stories at the One-Room School*. New York: Bantam Skylark, 1992.

Though this book is written for older children, it makes a good read aloud to younger children also. Dad tells his daughter and niece numerous stories of what it was like growing up in a one-room schoolhouse in Nutbrush, Mo. Dad's Aunt Daisy was the schoolteacher.

Tews, Susan. *The Gingerbread Doll*. New York: Clarion, 1993.

It was 1930 and a very hard year for her family, but Rebecca still wishes for a beautiful porcelain doll for Christmas. Though she does not get her porcelain doll, Mama shows her love by making a handmade gingerbread doll with clothing.

Tusa, Tricia. *The Family Reunion*. New York: Farrar Straus Giroux, 1993.

A strictly hilarious story describing what happens one year when the Beneada family members go to the wrong house for their family reunion.

Williams, Sherley Anne. *Working Cotton*. San Diego, Calif.: Harcourt Brace, 1992.

Young Shelan goes with her family every day to pick cotton but she is too young to pick herself.

Williams, Vera B. *A Chair for My Mother*. New York: Mulberry, 1982.

After a fire destroys all their furniture, a young girl's waitress mother and grandmother save all their coins in a large jar until it is full and they can afford to buy a new, overstuffed chair.

FIGURE 6.2 Fascinating Family Folklore

Contact Person: Stephanie Gildone

Library: Conneaut Carnegie Public Library, Conneaut, Ohio

Description: The following program description was given to members of the library's summer reading club.

"Do you have a funny, scary, or exciting story about a relative or incident that everyone tells at family gatherings? Well, we are looking for just such stories to make a book entitled *Fascinating Family Folklore*. Help us compile this book by writing your original story on the attached form and return it to the library by Friday, July 16. Make this a family project. Sit down with Mom, Dad, Grandma or Grandpa. Ask them to share some family history with you! The completed books will be handed out at the 'Old Fashioned Country Jamboree' on July 31 at the Community Center. Please print, write, or type your story neatly. Be sure to attach your picture to the form. Before handling in your story, have Mom or Dad read it to make sure they approve! You must return the completed permission slip with your story."

A permission slip accompanied the form. The form had the child's name, school, grade, and title of story on top. Space was left for the child to include a photo. Some children included pictures of relatives mentioned in their story. The rest of the form had lines on the front and back for the child to write the family story. Over 40 forms including some from staff members and library board members were stapled together with a bright cover and back sheet to make a booklet. Booklets were reproduced on a photocopier (pictures reproduced well in black and white!) and were distributed to each child.

Some samples of family folklore:

1. Alex Ecklund, Kindergarten. "A little boy named Harry lived on a farm in Carroll County. One November morning his Mom was baking cookies, and needed a cup of sugar. His Grandma lived a mile down the dirt path road, so his Mom bundled him in his coat, boots, hat and mittens. She sent him on his way with a note asking for the sugar stuck in his mitten. She forgot one thing—it was the first day of hunting season. As Harry walked and heard the hunters' guns, he was scared and sucked his thumb. When Harry arrived at his Grandma's, the note was wet and she couldn't read it. After warming up and having cookies and milk, Harry walked home empty handed. He had his cookies, but no one at his house had cookies that day. Harry is my Grandpa Kail and this happened 77 years ago, when he was four years old."

2. Leah Tobias, Grade 1. "During the late 1800s my Great-Great Aunt Matilda Scott of Butler, Pennsylvania, was robbed by Jesse James, the famous outlaw. As the story goes, Mrs. Scott was a passenger on a train en route to Hot Springs, Arkansas, with her son. Sometime during the trip, Jesse James and four masked bandits boarded the train and robbed the passengers of money and valuable possessions. Aunt Matilda hid her valuable jewelry in her hairdo. My Grandmother Thomas has one of my Great Aunt's earrings from the robbery. Before Jesse and his gang left the train, Jesse asked the Conductor for a pencil and paper, on which he wrote, 'Five Men Robbed Train Load of 400 People.' He requested this note be given to the Editor of a St. Louis newspaper."

FIGURE 6.2 Continued

3. Jocelyn Lucie Belle Bartone, Grade 2. "My great-great-great grandmother once rescued two babies from a bear. It all happened about 100 years ago. My great-great-great grandparents went to Michigan, traveling on the Ohio River on a flatboat. My great-great-great grandmother, Charlotte, was the cook on the flatboat. They had their baby, my great-great grandmother, Alta Belle, with them, and there was another lady with a baby too. One day, the flatboat tied up on shore, and the ladies went to pick berries. They put the two babies on a blanket by a tree. When they came back with their berries, there was a big bear right there beside the babies. They were afraid the bear would eat the babies. But the bear saw the big bucket of berries and started eating berries instead of babies. Charlotte grabbed a big stick and began hitting the bear to scare it. The bear ran off, and they grabbed the babies and ran as fast as they could. They left the berries for the bear. And that is how Charlotte rescued the babies. This is a true story, told by my great-grandmother, Alta Belle's daughter, Lucy Brown."

4. Patrick Bartone, Grade 5. "My story is not a scary or funny one, but it is a family story that is true. My great-grandfather, Vincent H. Brown, was an inventor who worked for RCA in New York City. He invented or developed many things, including some TV picture tubes we use now. One thing he developed, back in the late 1920s, was radio pictures; that means, sending pictures by radio waves. This project was done between New York and England. When everything was ready to be tested, the picture of the King of England was sent from England to New York. My great-grandfather sent back the picture of a little girl, about four years old. It was my grandmother! So she helped make history by being the first American to have her picture sent by radio waves!"

5. Scotty Nyman, Grade 5. "My Great-Grandma Bennett is 89 years old. She told a funny story of her new dentures. The day she went to the dentist my Great-Grandpa Bennett drove her. He parked the car in front of the Five and Dime Store. Grandma's appointment was in an office upstairs from the store. After getting her new teeth she stopped back to the car to tell Grandpa that she was going into the store for a few minutes. Once in the store her new teeth began to gag her and make her feel sick. She ran out of the store, got into the car with her head down and mouth covered. Grandma said 'Hurry up, I think I'm going to be sick.' No answer. So she said it one more time and looked up. Come to find out she was in the wrong car with another man sitting at the wheel. She jumped out of the car and ran to her own car. When she got in, Grandpa said 'It figures, you get new teeth and right away you're trying to run off with another man.'"

RESOURCE BOOKS

There are several resource books that will be helpful when planning programs emphasizing family relationships and the sharing of family histories. Several that will be useful are listed here.

FIGURE 6.3 Resource Books

Akeret, Robert U. *Family Tales, Family Wisdom: How To Gather the Stories of a Lifetime and Share Them With Your Family.* New York: Morrow, 1991.

Burrell, Sherry. *Families.* Bridgeport, Conn.: First Teacher Press, 1991.

Cooper, Kay. *Where Did You Get Those Eyes?: A Guide To Discovering Your Family History.* New York: Walker, 1988.

Mabrey, D.L. *Tell Me About Yourself: How To Interview Anyone From Your Friends to Famous People.* Minneapolis, Minn.: Lerner Publications, 1985.

Moore, Robin. *Awakening the Hidden Storyteller: How To Build a Storytelling Tradition in Your Family.* Boston, MA.: Shambhala, 1991.

Pellowski, Anne. *Family Storytelling Handbook.* New York: Macmillan, 1987.

Zimmerman, Bill. *How To Tape Instant Oral Biographies: Recording Your Family's Life Story in Sound and Sight.* New York: Bantam, 1992.

THE USE OF MULTICULTURAL LITERATURE

There is no doubt that multiethnic and interracial families are no longer considered a minority in society, as in years past. According to the Census Bureau, by the year 2050 about half of the U.S. population will be non-European. From large metropolitan cities to the smallest rural towns, there are families with many different ethnic backgrounds. It is important that all children feel pride in their ethnic and racial identity. There is no reason why one race or ethnic background should be considered superior to another, yet both in schools and in public-library programs, the trend in the past has been to teach Eurocentric curriculums and to share holiday customs or programs that appeal to families of European heritage. It obviously was much more difficult in the past to find children's literature that represented people of different ethnic or racial backgrounds, and though that has been changing dramatically, there still is a long way to go. African-American literature particularly has been emphasized recently, but children's books depicting Hispanic or other Spanish-speaking populations, Asian-American children, and children from Middle-Eastern cultures, to mention just three, are much more scarce. Hopefully this will continue to improve in the future as demand increases and libraries continue to buy books representing different ethnic groups. If librarians demand and purchase these books, publishers will produce more of them.

There are still librarians reluctant to purchase materials or consider changing their programs for children because they feel that Caucasian children with European roots are the majority in their neighborhood. Even if this is true (and it may be that because the library has nothing to offer other children, they are not coming to the library), it is still important to learn about other cultural groups. To counter racism in our society, it is important that even young children obtain an awareness of other cultural traditions and different ways of life. Children need to realize what physical and cultural characteristics they have in common with other children, and what physical and cultural differences they have. They need to realize that children all over the world share many of the same feelings. They need to learn to respect each other and their ideas, and be tolerant of each other. One of the best ways to do this is through the use of multicultural literature. It is important, however, to use multicultural literature year-round and as part of every program. Books should be included into programs naturally. There are many picture books that depict children from different ethnic backgrounds that can be used in storytimes. Folk tales from around the world can be incorporated without any special planning. Ethnic songs, finger plays, and art activities can be added at any time of the year. What is important is not to organize activities just around holidays. For example, do not use African-American literature, art activities, and songs only during "Black History Month" in February. Do not share books and activities on Chinese children only in January for Chinese New Year. Literature and activities involving different ethnic groups should be included regularly throughout the year. This is true for every library, regardless of the ethnic group that is in the majority in the area, and programming and literature depicting and recognizing all ethnic groups should be included.

Librarians might want to look at two resources that early childhood educators consider important when teaching young children. The National Association for the Education of Young Children has published *Anti-Bias Curriculum: Tools for Empowering Young Children* and *Valuing Diversity: The Primary Years.*[2] Several points made in these guides are useful for librarians to remember:

1. Avoid reading only one book about a certain cultural group just once a year, or offering only one cultural program around a holiday. This is tokenism.

2. Avoid reading books about children of color only on special occasions or for certain holidays.
3. Avoid stereotypes in literature. Examples are books depicting Native Americans wearing feathered headdresses, books depicting Native American children in the past only, books depicting African children as poor and living in villages, books showing children in costumes rather than traditional dress, or books showing quaint customs of a country. If you use books about a certain country, such as Japan, make sure that children do not get the impression that this is what Japanese-American children are like who were born and raised in the United States.

If you share a certain book that you feel has an excellent plot and much appeal for children, (the perfect example is *Amazing Grace* by Mary Hoffman, Dial, 1991) explain to children later that not all Native Americans wore feathered headdresses, and that when they were worn, they were for ceremonial purposes. Another example that may be difficult to explain, and might be better left unshared is *Country Far Away* by Nigel Gray (Orchard, 1989). In this book a child in urban America is compared to a child in a village in Africa. Obviously there are many cities in Africa, and many rural areas in America. To compare urban America to rural Africa is not really fair and will lead many children to believe that all African children are poor and live in villages. If you share this book you will need to point out that the comparison made in the book is not of two similarly populated areas in different countries, but rather it attempts to compare two dissimilar areas.

It is not always easy to know whether a book depicts an accurate and fair portrayal of a country or ethnic group. Reviews are very important when making purchasing considerations, but even reviewers sometimes do not recognize stereotypes or myths that have become accepted in our culture over the years.

There are various types of multicultural literature that can be naturally introduced in programs. Probably the easiest way is to use multicultural folk tales. Another idea is to share books where the setting is incidental and the themes and characters have universal appeal. These books depict a mixture of children, both white and of color, interacting normally. An example is the African-American child depicted in *Mary Had a Little Lamb* by Sarah Josepha Hale, illustrated by Bruce McMillan (Scholastic, 1990). A third idea is to share books that show cultural diversity, children from other cultures coming to America, or what life is like for children in other countries.

MULTICULTURAL FAMILY PROGRAMMING

The following are just a few ideas to consider so that your library family programs are more multicultural in nature.

Music, Art Activities and Games: Incorporate music from different countries and cultural groups in your programs. Do not suggest that the music is different, exotic, or foreign. Use some musical instruments and allow children to try instruments that are not as common to them, such as thumb pianos. You can also share different types of art activities and cooperative, noncompetitive games from different countries. Consult the resource books at the end of this section for ideas (see Fig. 6.5).

Pen Pals: Arrange for children to write to pen pals in other countries or even other places in the United States.

Family Days: Have families talk about their own cultures or traditions during family programs. They may bring objects or food to share. If you want more cultural diversity than what your audience represents, invite specific speakers.

Holidays: Consider displaying books and posters each month that represent the different holidays of different cultures. For example, in December include holidays such as Kwanzaa, Hanukkah, and Las Posadas in addition to Christmas. If you do have a holiday celebration, such as Chinese New Year, make sure this is not the only time you read books, play music, or do activities related to Chinese culture.

Storytime or Program Themes: If you are doing a theme on a certain subject, such as "Houses and Homes," make sure you remember that there are different types of houses and homes around the world. Share a book that will depict some of these, such as *This is My House,* by Arthur Dorros (Scholastic, 1992). If you are presenting a program on a certain country, do not treat just one area of difference such as food. Point out similarities and differences between homes, clothing, food, school, celebrations, etc.

Folk Tales: Include folk tales from different countries whenever possible. You may wish to point out the country where the folk tale originated from on the globe first.

Multicultural Family Stories: Use multicultural family stories whenever possible in family programming. In addition to the ones mentioned in the previous bibliography (see Fig. 6.1) in this chapter on family stories, consider some of these that follow.

FIGURE 6.4 Multicultural Family Stories

Family Life for Children in Other Countries

Baer, Edith. *This Is the Way We Go to School.* New York: Scholastic, 1990.

This describes all the different ways children travel to school.

Cowen-Fletcher, Jane. *It Takes a Village.* New York: Scholastic, 1994.

In the West African village of Benin, Yemi tells her mother that she will watch her little brother Kokou, but her mother knows better. The African proverb, "It takes a whole village to raise a child," comes true in this story.

Dorros, Arthur. *This Is My House.* New York: Scholastic, 1992.

Different types of houses families live in from different countries of the world are depicted. The words "This is my house" are written in thirteen different languages.

Heide, Florence Parry. *The Day of Ahmed's Secret.* New York: Lothrop, Lee & Shepard, 1990.

A boy has a special secret he wishes to share with his family after his day's work of hauling butane gas canisters for his family's business. His secret—he has learned to write his name in Arabic.

Heide, Florence Parry. *Sami and the Time of the Troubles.* New York: Clarion, 1992.

The life of a ten-year-old boy and his Lebanese family during present-day war times show the family living both above ground and underground in a basement shelter, to avoid bombing.

Isadora, Rachel. *At the Crossroads.* New York: Greenwillow, 1991.

Families, living in the segregated townships of South Africa, do not see their fathers who work in the mines for months at a time. Here children stand at the crossroads, anxiously awaiting their fathers' return.

Isadora, Rachel. *Over the Green Hills.* New York: Greenwillow, 1992.

Zolani and his mother live on the rural east coast of South Africa and are going on a journey to visit his grandmother.

Levinson, Riki. *Our Home Is the Sea.* New York: Dutton, 1988.

A young Chinese boy from Hong Kong describes why he loves living on the sea and why he wants to be a fisherman like his father and grandfather.

Lewin, Hugh. *Jafta: The Homecoming.* New York: Knopf, 1994.

A young black South African boy relates how he feels about his father's homecoming after working for months in the city.

Lewin, Ted. *Amazon Boy.* New York: Macmillan, 1993.

Paulo's father gives him a special birthday gift—they will take the overnight steamer down the Amazon to the great city of Belem—where Paulo has never been before.

FIGURE 6.4 Continued

Margolies, Barbara. *Kanu of Kathmandu.* New York:Four Winds Press, 1992.

Eight-year-old Kanu goes with his father and his friends on a tour of several small cities and villages outside of Nepal's capital city where Kanu lives.

Margolies, Barbara. *Rehema's Journey.* New York:Scholastic, 1990.

Nine-year-old Rehema leaves her rural home in Tanzania for the first time and travels with her father to Arusha City and the Ngorongoro Crater.

Mennen, Ingrid and Niki Daly. *Somewhere in Africa.* New York: Dutton, 1990.

This story about a young boy named Asharaf conveys what it is like to live in an African city.

Mitchell, Rita. *Hue Boy.* New York: Dial, 1993.

All of Hue Boy's family and friends living in the Caribbean worry because it seems that Hue Boy will never grow in size.

Morris, Ann. *Bread, Bread, Bread.* New York: Lothrop, Lee & Shepard, 1989. Also, *Hats, Hats, Hats; Houses and Homes; Loving; On the Go; Tools,* and several others.

A series of easy nonfiction books with wonderful photographs depicting families in different countries engaged in everyday activities. Each book has an index showing in which country each photo was taken along with a brief description of each photo.

Stock, Catherine. *Where Are You Going Manyoni?* New York: Morrow, 1993.

Manyoni walks for miles through rural Zimbabwe and past wild animals to reach her school.

Williams, Karen Lynn. *Galimoto.* New York: Lothrop, Lee & Shepard, 1990.

Kondi finds enough wire to shape into a galimoto—a toy car enjoyed by African children.

Children Growing Up in America With Dual Cultures

Ancona, George. *Powwow.* San Diego, Calif.: Harcourt Brace, 1993.

This book celebrates families coming together in friendship to share the traditions of a powwow.

Brown, Tricia. *Hello, Amigos!* New York: Holt, 1986.

Frankie Valdez celebrates his birthday with his family and friends in San Francisco's Mission District with a corona, a mariachi, and a pinata.

Brown, Tricia. *Lee Ann: The Story of a Vietnamese-American Girl.* New York: Putnam, 1991.

Lee Ann's family fled Vietnam from a refugee camp in Malaysia and now live in America. In this book, they celebrate Te't, the Vietnamese New Year.

Garza, Carmen Lomas. *Family Pictures.* Chicago: Children's Book Press, 1990.

A bilingual text and illustrations depict the author's family and her experiences growing up Hispanic in Kingsville, Texas, near the Mexican border. Among her many memories are ''Los Posados,'' pinatas, cakewalks, and picking nopal cactus.

FIGURE 6.4 Continued

Hewett, Joan. *Hector Lives in the United States Now.* New York: Lippincott, 1990.

> Ten-year-old Hector Almaraz, born in Guadalajara, Mexico, now lives in Los Angeles. Two special events in Hector's life are covered: his first Communion and his parents' decision to apply for citizenship under the provisions of a new immigration law.

Hoyt, Goldsmith, Diane. *Cherokee Summer.* New York: Holiday, 1993.

> Ten-year-old Bridget describes her Cherokee family life and such events as a Hog Fry, a stomp dance, weaving baskets with her grandmother from honeysuckle vines, and hunting crawdads in the creek with her family. The Trail of Tears is also described.

Howlett, Bud. *I'm New Here.* Boston: Houghton Mifflin, 1993.

> Jazmin's family has just moved to the United States from El Salvador and it is her first day of school. She speaks no English and feels out of place but her supportive family and a new friend help her.

Hoyt, Goldsmith, Diane. *Hoang Anh: A Vietnamese-American Boy.* New York: Holiday, 1992.

> Hoang Anh's family escaped Vietnam on a fishing boat. Though he lives like most of his friends, his special Vietnamese heritage is celebrated also. Described is Te't season.

Keegan, Marcia. *Pueblo Boy: Growing Up in Two Worlds.* New York: Cobblehill, 1991.

> Ten-year-old Timmy Roybal, a Pueblo Indian living in New Mexico, uses a computer at school and plays baseball, but also learns the customs of his ancestors, including the corn dance.

Kendall, Russ. *Eskimo Boy.* New York: Scholastic, 1992.

> Seven-year-old Norman Kokeok, an Inupiaq Eskimo boy, lives with his family in a small Alaskan village. There is ice fishing, dogsled racing, festivals, and summer, with 23 hours of daylight.

Kuklin, Susan. *How My Family Lives in America.* New York: Bradbury, 1992.

> Sanu who is African-American, Eric who is Hispanic-American, and April who is Asian-American, each describes family life in America.

Waters, Kate. *Lion Dancer.* New York: Scholastic, 1990.

> Six-year-old Ernie Wan lives in Chinatown in New York City. This is the first year he will perform in the Chinese New Year's celebration in the Lion Dance.

Children From America Living in Other Countries

Gordon, Ginger. *My Two Worlds.* New York: Clarion, 1993.

> Kirsty Rodriguez, from New York City, spends Christmas with her relatives in Puerto Plata in the Dominican Republic, and also celebrates her eighth birthday.

Kroll, Virginia. *Masai and I.* New York: Four Winds, 1992.

> An American girl, Linda, studies East Africa in school and imagines what her life would be like as a Masai, including going to her grandmother's 70th birthday party.

FIGURE 6.4 Continued

Leigh, Nila K. *Learning To Swim in Swaziland: A Child's Eye-View of a Southern African Country.* New York: Scholastic, 1993.

Nila was eight when her parents took her to live for a year in Swaziland in southern Africa. This book is a series of letters written to her classmates back in New York City.

Trivas, Irene. *Annie . . . Anya: A Month in Moscow.* New York: Orchard, 1992.

Five-year-old Annie goes to live in Russia for a month with her doctor parents who are working for a month in a Russian hospital. She is not very happy until she meets Anya at a day care center.

Williams, Karen Lynn. *When Africa Was Home.* New York: Orchard, 1991.

Peter is raised in Africa from infancy and misses it, his friends, and nanny, when his family decide to move to America. Later his father again finds a job in Africa and the family moves back "to home" as Peter describes it.

Family Celebrations or Holidays

Ancona, George. *Pablo Remembers.* New York: Lothrop, Lee & Shepard, 1993.

Pablo realizes that the three-day fiesta of the Day of the Dead will be especially important to his family this year since his grandmother died and they miss her very much.

Chocolate, Deborah. *My First Kwanzaa Book.* New York: Scholastic, 1992.

A simple picture book describing the African-American celebration of Kwanzaa, from the East African Swahili meaning "the first" and being celebrated from the day after Christmas until the first day of the New Year. Included is a glossary on the seven principles of Kwanzaa and definitions of symbols and words used during Kwanzaa.

Czernecki, Stefan and Timothy Rhodes. *Pancho's Pinata.* New York: Hyperion, 1992.

Pancho rescues a beautiful star that is ensnared on top of a cactus on Christmas Eve in his Mexican village.

Delacre, Lulu. *Vejigante.* New York: Scholastic, 1993.

Ramon has secretly put together his own vejigante costume for Carnival during the 28 days of February without his family knowing, but runs into an unexpected problem when a goat rips it beyond repair.

Drucker, Malka. *A Jewish Holiday ABC.* San Diego, Calif.: Harcourt Brace, 1992.

This alphabet book introduces young children to various Jewish holidays.

Joseph, Lynn. *An Island Christmas.* Clarion, 1992.

Families celebrate together during Christmas on the islands of Trinidad and Tobago. Rosie helps Mama in the kitchen making gifts for everyone.

Kimmelman, Leslie. *Hanukkah Lights, Hanukkah Nights.* New York: HarperCollins, 1992. Also, Manushkin, Fran. *Latkes and Applesauce: A Hanukkah Story.* New York: Scholastic, 1990. Schotter, Roni. *Hanukkah!* Boston: Little, Brown, 1990.

All three books show families sharing the special season of Hanukkah.

FIGURE 6.4 Continued

Pinkney, Andrea Davis. *Seven Candles for Kwanzaa.* New York: Dial, 1993.

This is a beautifully illustrated book describing the origins and practices of the seven-day American holiday inspired by African traditions in which people of African descent rejoice in their ancestral values. Also, Hoyt-Goldsmith, Diane. *Celebrating Kwanzaa.* New York: Holiday, 1993.

Say, Allen. *Tree of Cranes.* Boston: Houghton Mifflin, 1991.

A young Japanese boy has never heard of Christmas but his mother, who was born in California, decides one year to share with him the tradition she remembers from her childhood. They decorate a tree with candles and origami cranes, and the boy receives a kite for a present.

Soto, Gary. *Too Many Tamales.* New York: Putnam, 1993.

A Christmas family get-together is almost ruined when Maria and her cousins lose Maria's mother's diamond ring while making tamales.

Multicultural Poetry For Families

Clark, Ann Nolan. *In My Mother's House.* New York: Viking, 1991.

The world of Tewa children of Tesuque Pueblo, New Mexico, is shared through poetry about their world.

Delacre, Lulu. *Arroz con Leche: Popular Songs and Rhymes from Latin America.* New York: Scholastic, 1989.

This is a collection of songs and rhymes from Central and South America.

Feelings, Tom. *Soul Looks Back in Wonder.* New York: Dial, 1993.

Tom Feelings' dramatic artwork accompanies a collection of poems by such famous African American writers as Maya Angelou, Lucille Clifton, Langston Hughes, Walter Dean Myers, and Askia M. Toure.

Greenfield, Eloise. *Night on Neighborhood Street.* New York: Dial, 1991.

The sights, sounds and strengths of family life in a African-American neighborhood are shared through poetry.

Gunning, Monica. *Not a Copper Penny in Me House.* Honesdale, Pa.: Boyds Mills Press, 1993.

A young child's life in the Caribbean is described through poetry.

Hudson, Wade. *Pass It On: African-American Poetry for Children.* New York: Scholastic, 1993.

This collection of poetry by well-known African-American poets concerns family life and play, but also serious subjects. The hope is to preserve the oral tradition by "passing on" the poetry.

Jones, Hettie, selector. *The Trees Stand Shining.* Reissued. New York: Dial, 1993.

Songs of Native Americans translated from the Indian languages are enhanced by paintings executed by a Caldecott Honor artist.

Joseph, Lynn. *Coconut Kind of Day.* New York: Lothrop, Lee & Shepard, 1990.

Poems reflecting a Caribbean rhythm describe the sights, sounds, and tastes of Trinidad through a young native girl.

FIGURE 6.4 Continued

Myers, Walter Dean. *Brown Angels: An Album of Pictures and Verse.*

Turn-of-the-century photographs of African-American children are accompanied by poems by this famous African-American writer.

Strickland, Dorothy S. and Michael R. Strickland. *Families: Poems Celebrating the African American Experience.* Honesdale, Pa.: Boyds Mills Press, 1994.

This anthology celebrates family relationships in diverse African-American families.

Thomas, Joyce Carol. *Brown Honey in Broomwheat Tea.* New York: HarperCollins, 1993.

Poems of family, individuality, and pride of heritage expressed by an African-American girl and accompanied by Floyd Cooper's luminous paintings.

Yolen, Jane, ed. *Sleep Rhymes Around the World.* Honesdale, Pa.: Boyds Mills Press, 1994. Also, *Street Rhymes Around the World* by the same editor.

Twenty-one delightful sleep rhymes from 17 nations and republics are presented in their native language, along with a translation in English. The book is illustrated by 17 international artists.

INTERGENERATIONAL PROGRAMMING

The National Council on the Aging defines intergenerational programs as those between any two generations that involve the sharing of knowledge or experience between young and old. Thus libraries providing family library programming are doing intergenerational programming. However, when most libraries speak of intergenerational programs, they consider grandparents, aunts, uncles, or elderly neighbors or seniors involved with young children in addition to or instead of the caregivers.

An excellent resource to use when planning intergenerational programming is Rhea Rubin's *Intergenerational Programming: A How-To-Do-It Manual for Librarians* (Neal-Schuman, 1993). There is much information on model programs and resource materials.

Following are some intergenerational programs involving young children and older people (other then their caregivers) that have been successful in public libraries.

Grandparents as Storytellers or Readers: Many libraries have successfully involved grandparents as readers or storytellers to

---

FIGURE 6.5 Resource Books Helpful in Planning Multicultural Programs

Allen, Judy, Earldene McNeill, and Velma Schmidt. *Cultural Awareness for Children.* Menlo Park, Calif.: Addison-Wesley, 1992.

Caballero, Jane. *Children Around the World Today.* Atlanta: Humanics Learning, 1992.

Hayden, Carla D. *Venture Into Cultures.* Chicago: American Library Association, 1992.

Kear, Dr. Dennis J., and Dr. Jeri A. Carroll. *A Multicultural Guide to Literature-Based Whole Language Activities for Young Children.* Carthage, Ill.: Good Apple, 1993.

Labyn, Carole L. and Lois S. Webb. *Multicultural Cookbook for Students.* Phoenix, Ariz.: Oryx, 1993.

Lipman, Doug. *We All Go Together: Creative Activities for Children to Use With Multicultural Folksongs.* Phoenix, Ariz.: Oryx, 1993.

MacDonald, Margaret Read. *Look Back and See: Twenty Lively Tales for Gentle Tellers.* New York: H.W.Wilson Company, 1991.

McKinnon, Elizabeth. *Special Day Celebrations.* Everett, Wash.: Warren, 1989.

Milord, Susan. *Hands Around the World: 365 Creative Ways to Build Cultural Awareness and Global Respect.* Charlotte, Vt.: Williamson Publishing, 1992.

Moore, Jo Ellen. *Families Around the World.* Monterey, Calif.: Evan-Moor, 1991.

Pellowski, Anne. *The Story Vine: A Sourcebook of Unusual and Easy-To-Tell Stories From Around the World.* New York: Macmillan, 1984.

Shannon, George. *More Stories to Solve: Fifteen Folktales From Around the World.* New York: Greenwillow, 1990.

Shannon, George. *Stories to Solve: Folktales From Around the World.* New York: Greenwillow, 1985.

Sierra, Judy. *Fantastic Theatre.* New York: H.W.Wilson Company, 1991. (30 plays from around the world).

Sierra, Judy and Robert Kaminski. *Twice Upon a Time: Stories to Tell, Retell, Act Out, and Write About.* New York: H.W. Wilson Company, 1989.

Sierra, Judy. *Flannel Board Storytelling Book.* New York: H.W. Wilson Company, 1987.

Sierra, Judy and Robert Kaminski. *Multicultural Folktales: Stories to Tell Young Children.* Phoenix, Ariz.: Oryx, 1991.

Terzian, Alexandra M. *Kids' Multicultural Art Book.* Charlotte, Vt.: Williamson Publishing, 1992.

Warren, Jean. *Small World Celebrations.* Everett, Wash.: Warren, 1988.

---

young children. Librarians first train these volunteers how to select books, how to read to young children, and how to present stories. These volunteers are asked to commit to presenting a certain number of programs at the library, normally after school hours. Not only do the young children benefit, but the seniors who volunteer find the program a very rewarding use of their time.

Grandparents' Kits: Some libraries have prepared kits to circulate, based on children's interest levels or ages, so that grandparents can read at their leisure to young children. Often kits will not only contain books, but also a cassette, hand puppet, tip sheets, etc.

Grandparents as Invited Guests to Storytimes or Programs: Libraries often make a special effort to invite grandparents as guests to story programs or other special programs. Though this is a wonderful idea, it is important to advertise the program in a way not to slight children who do not have a grandparent or whose grandparent(s) live far away. Make sure the invitation is to a "grandparent, honorary grandparent, or a special older friend." Several intergenerational or family stories are usually presented (see Fig. 6.6). You may want these visitors to tell stories of when they were young to primary age children and bring something for show and tell if possible!

Pen Pal Projects: To extend the literacy experience and involve children with writing, several libraries have instituted pen-pal projects. Older library patrons have corresponded with younger patrons who are able to write their own letters. These older library patrons can be recruited from mail-a-book programs, home-bound services, or other senior-citizens groups that meet at the library.

Children's Programs at Senior Citizen Centers: Some libraries have had success by holding children's programs at senior-citizen centers. Children enjoy participation stories, sing songs, and participate in art or craft projects, assisted by seniors. Obviously this type of program requires coordination with senior-citizen agencies, but the resulting programs can be very rewarding for both the children and seniors.

Senior Tutors: For young primary grade children that need assistance with homework, libraries have senior volunteers tutor the students after school at the library.

Outreach to Head Start Centers or Preschools: For librarians pressed for time to do outreach to Head Start or early childhood centers, seniors can be trained in storytelling skills at the library, then volunteer to do programming once a month at centers. Though librarians need to take the time to train the volunteers, the number of centers that can be reached through these senior volunteers far outnumber the contacts that can be made by one librarian.

FIGURE 6.6 Intergenerational Stories

(Other intergenerational stories may be found in the bibliographies in this chapter on "Family Storytimes That Depict Family Life" and "Multicultural Family Stories.")

Ackerman, Karen. *Song and Dance Man.* New York: Knopf, 1988.

> Grandpa unpacks items from a cedar chest in the attic and demonstrates to his grandchildren how he was a "song and dance" man (vaudeville entertainer) when he was younger. (1989 Caldecott Medal.)

Addy, Sharon Hart. *Visit with Great-Grandma.* Morton Grove, Ill.: Albert Whitman & Co., 1989.

> Great-Grandmother speaks very little English but Barbara and she still share special moments making strawberry kolach, looking at photographs, and talking about "the old country."

Ballard, Robin. *Granny and Me.* New York: Greenwillow, 1992.

> A young girl describes the special times she has with her Granny, especially looking at the family photo album.

Beil, Karen Magnuson. *Grandma According to Me.* New York: Doubleday, 1992.

> A young girl describes why her Grandmother is so wonderful—even with all her wrinkles, or story lines, as her young granddaughter calls them.

Bonners, Susan. *Wooden Doll.* New York: Lothrop, Lee & Shepard, 1991.

> A young girl's grandfather, who left his native Poland at age 17 never to return again, has only his mother's wooden stacking doll to remind him of his homeland.

Buckley, Helen E. *Grandfather and I.* New York: Lothrop, Lee & Shepard, 1994.

> A young child explains why Grandfather is the perfect person to spend time with—he is never in a hurry! Also by the same author, *Grandmother and I.*

Bunting, Eve. *Sunshine Home.* New York: Clarion, 1994.

> After Timmie's Gram falls and breaks her hip, she is put in the "Sunshine Home" where the family goes to visit her. Both his parents and Gram try to pretend that it is okay and they are happy about the decision, but Timmie finds out that is not true.

Bunting, Eve. *Wednesday Surprise.* New York: Clarion, 1989.

> Anna teaches Grandma to read when they are together on Wednesday nights and they surprise the rest of the family with the secret on Dad's birthday.

Caseley, Judith. *Apple Pie and Onions.* New York: Greenwillow, 1987.

> Rebecca's grandmother (who came from Russia on a boat) tells stories of her life when she first arrived in America. Rebecca becomes embarrassed when her Grandma speaks very loud in Yiddish to a friend.

Caseley, Judith. *Dear Annie.* New York: Greenwillow, 1991.

> The text is a series of letters between Anna and her pen pal, her Grandpa.

Castle, Caroline and Peter Bowman. *Grandpa Baxter and the Photographs.* New York: Orchard, 1993.

> Grandpa Baxter and Benjamin Bear share Great-Granddad Dudley's photograph collection and talk about family history.

FIGURE 6.6 Continued

Cech, John. *My Grandmother's Journey.* New York: Bradbury, 1991.

Korie's Grandmother describes her life in Russia, her many hardships, and meeting gypsies until she finally arrived in the United States after World War II.

Choi, Sook Nyul. *Halmoni and the Picnic.* Boston: Houghton Mifflin, 1993.

Yunmi wants to help her recently immigrated Korean Grandmother fit in with American ways so she volunteers her to be a chaperon at her third grade picnic.

Daly, Niki. *Not So Fast Songololo.* New York: Atheneum, 1986.

Malusi and his Gogo (Granny) go shopping in the city (in Africa) and Gogo spends some of her last money on buying him a new pair of red tackies. Malusi normally only has hand-me-downs to wear.

Denslow, Sharon Phillips. *At Taylor's Place.* New York: Bradbury, 1990.

Tory likes to visit her neighbor Taylor's workshop where she helps him complete another of his woodcarving projects. (This author has several other intergenerational titles.)

DePaola, Tomie. *Now One Foot, Now the Other.* New York: G.P. Putnam, 1981.

Grandfather Bob teaches Bobby how to walk when he is young and the two become best friends. After Grandpa suffers a stroke, it is Bobby who must teach Grandpa how to walk again.

Dionetti, Michelle. *Coal Mine Peaches.* New York: Orchard, 1991.

A granddaughter fondly recalls the stories her grandfather told so many times—of his coal mining days, building the Brooklyn Bridge, and other family stories.

DiSalvo-Ryan, DyAnne. *Uncle Willie and the Soup Kitchen.* New York: Morrow, 1991.

A young boy spends a day with his Uncle Willie to find out why anyone would want to work in a soup kitchen preparing meals for those who are hungry.

Dodds, Siobhan. *Grandpa Bud.* Cambridge, Mass.: Candlewick Press, 1993.

Polly telephones Grandpa several times to tell him about various friends she is bringing along with her when she comes to visit and what food they like. Grandpa keeps making more and more food, only to find out that Polly's friends are stuffed animals.

Dorros, Arthur. *Abuela.* New York: Dutton, 1991.

While riding on a bus with her Abuela (grandmother), a young girl imagines they are flying together over the city of New York. The sights they see are described in English with some Spanish phrases.

Edmiston, Jim and Jane Ross. *Little Eagle Lots of Owls.* Boston: Houghton Mifflin, 1993.

Grandfather gives Little Eagle Lots of Owls a gift of a strange animal that does not want to wake up. At nightfall, he discovers the one animal is actually three owls, and he now understands how he received his name.

Gilman, Phoebe. *Something From Nothing.* New York: Scholastic, 1992.

In this traditional Jewish folktale, Joseph's Grandpa transforms Joseph's baby blanket into even smaller items as he grows older until nothing is left.

FIGURE 6.6 Continued

Greenfield, Eloise. *Grandpa's Face.* New York: Philomel, 1988.

Grandpa makes a mean face while rehearsing for a play and Tamika is afraid he will look at her in that mean way in the future.

Greenfield, Eloise. *William and the Good Old Days.* New York: HarperCollins, 1993.

William wants the good old days back before his beloved Grandma became sick and started losing her sight.

Grifalconi, Ann. *Osa's Pride.* Boston: Little, Brown, 1990.

Osa, who lives in a small village in Africa, brags about her father who died in a war, which causes her to lose her friends. Her Grandma shares a story about pride in a colorful story cloth she is making.

Grifalconi, Ann. *The Village of Round and Square Houses.* Boston: Little, Brown, 1986.

Osa's grandmother tells her why in her village the men live in square houses and the women live separately in round ones. This village really exists in the remote hills of Cameroon.

Griffith, Helen. *Grandaddy and Janetta.* New York: Greenwillow, 1993.

Five short chapters describe Janetta's trip to Grandaddy's place, which she has not visited for a year. Grandaddy has not changed any, but Janetta finds there have been some other changes on the farm, including new kittens.

Hennessy, B.G. *When You Were Just a Little Girl.* New York: Viking, 1991.

In poetic verse, Grandma describes the games and activities from her youth.

Hest, Amy. *Fancy Aunt Jess.* New York: Morrow, 1990.

A young girl loves having sleepovers with her fancy Aunt Jess who lives in Brooklyn.

Hest, Amy. *The Purple Coat.* New York: Four Winds Press, 1986.

Gabby begs her Grandfather, who is a tailor, to make her a purple coat this year instead of the normal navy one she gets every year, even though it is against her mother's wishes.

Hines, Anna Grossnickle. *Gramma's Walk.* New York: Greenwillow, 1993.

Gramma, in a wheelchair, and Donnie go on an imaginary walk to the seashore and envision everything they see and do there.

Johnson, Angela. *When I Am Old With You.* New York: Orchard, 1990.

A young girl shares old pictures of the family with her granddaddy and imagines what it would be like to be old like him.

Kimmelman, Leslie. *Me and Nana.* New York: Harper & Row, 1990.

When Nana comes to visit, Natalie and she have very special outings.

Levinson, Riki. *I Go With My Family to Grandma's.* New York: Dutton, 1986.

This tells how five cousins and their families, each from a different borough of New York City, travel to Grandma's at the turn of the century. Also by the same author, *Watch the Stars Come Out.*

FIGURE 6.6 Continued

Linden, Ann Marie. *One Smiling Grandma.* New York: Dial, 1992.

A young girl and her grandmother's life on a Caribbean island are described in this counting book for young children.

Martin, Bill. *Knots on a Counting Rope.* New York: Holt, 1987.

Boy-Strength-of-Blue-Horses, who is blind, has his grandfather tell him the story of his birth and about a horse race he participated in when he was older, as his grandfather adds another knot on the counting rope.

Miller, Montazalee. *My Grandmother's Cookie Jar.* Los Angeles: Price Stern Sloan, 1987.

A grandmother tells her grandchild stories from the family's history of life long ago. After her grandmother's death, it is the granddaughter's turn to share stories from her Native American heritage.

Mora, Pat. *A Birthday Basket for Tia.* New York: Macmillan, 1992.

Cecilia gives her Great-Aunt a basket for her birthday filled with items that will remind her of the special times they have together.

Oberman, Sheldon. *The Always Prayer Shawl.* Honesdale, Pa.: Boyds Mills Press, 1994.

Adam, a young Jewish boy in Czarist Russia, must leave the country with his family and without his Grandfather, who gives him his prayer shawl, which in turn had been given to him by his Grandfather. Adam later has his own grandchild and he tells the family story as he also gives him the shawl.

Patrick, Denise Lewis. *Red Dancing Shoes.* New York: Tambourine, 1993.

A young girl receives a gift of the finest, reddest, shiniest shoes ever from her Grandmama and goes to show them to her favorite Aunt. When she falls in the mud and dirties the new shoes, she despairs, but her Aunt comes to the rescue.

Polacco, Patricia. *Chicken Sunday.* New York: Philomel, 1992.

To make money to buy Stewart and Winston's "Gramma," Miss Eula, a special hat, a young girl teaches them how to decorate eggs to sell, the way her bubbie from the old country taught her to do.

Polacco, Patricia. *Mrs. Katz and Tush.* New York: Bantam, 1992.

Larnel becomes friends with his neighbor, Mrs. Katz, through an abandoned kitten. Mrs. Katz shares stories of her Jewish heritage which he relates to his black history. The two celebrate Passover Seder together.

Say, Allen. *My Grandfather's Journey.* Boston: Houghton Mifflin, 1993.

The author tells the story of his Grandfather who moves from Japan to California, and after many years, moves back because of missing his homeland so much. Later the grandson moves the same way and finds he also misses his homeland, thus better understanding his Grandfather's stories. (1994 Caldecott)

Stevenson, James. *Could Be Worse.* New York: Greenwillow, 1977.

Grandpa overhears his grandchildren say that nothing interesting happens to him, so the next day he tells them about the most incredible adventure that happened to him. This is one of a series of books about Grandpa's tall tales.

FIGURE 6.6 Continued

Stolz, Mary. *Storm in the Night.* New York: HarperCollins, 1988.

During a terrible thunderstorm, Thomas hears stories from his grandfather's boyhood and about how he was also terrified of thunderstorms.

Strangis, Joel. *Grandfather's Rock.* Boston: Houghton Mifflin, 1993.

An Italian folktale describes how a poor family finds a way to keep an elderly Grandfather living with them instead of in a home for the elderly.

Waddell, Martin. *Grandma's Bill.* New York: Orchard, 1990.

Grandma shares pictures and stories from a photo album with young Bill. When he questions who the one man is, he hears about his grandfather, also named Bill.

Widman, Christine. *The Lemon Drop Jar.* New York: Macmillan, 1992.

Great-Aunt Emma tells stories about her past and how her lemon drop jar reminds her of her mother.

Williams, David. *Grandma Essie's Covered Wagon.* New York: Knopf, 1993.

The author's Grandma Essie tells the story of how her family left Missouri by covered wagon to Kansas for a better life, but after losing everything to a drought, moved to Oklahoma and later back to Missouri.

Family-History Projects: Though this topic was discussed earlier in this chapter, this is a reminder that young children can interview grandparents or other seniors about their life histories or what it was like for them growing up.

Bifolkal Kits: Bifolkal Productions, Inc. (809 Williamson St., Madison, WI 53703), a nonprofit corporation, sells Bifolkal Kits, each of which revolves around a topic and is designed for older adults to relive memories and share past experiences with children. Kits contain numerous items, many multisensory, such as slides, songs, audio tapes, skits, jokes, things to touch and feel, scratch and sniff items, recipes, large-print poems, and a programming guide. Examples of kits include: Remembering automobiles; Remembering farm days; Remembering music; Remembering county fairs; Remembering fashion; Remembering school days; Remembering fun and games; Remembering work life; and Remembering pets.

Senior Volunteers for Children's Programs: Many libraries have used senior volunteers to help with programming details or extras, such as making name tags for storytimes; making cushions for children to sit on during storytimes; making flannel-or magnetic-board kits for librarians; or assisting with art and craft projects.

There are various local organizations that can be contacted when planning library programs that will involve seniors. In addition to checking with nursing homes and senior-citizen centers that are provided with books by the library, other organizations include Retired Senior Volunteer Programs (RSVP); Volunteers in Service to America (VISTA); local literacy coalitions; Foster Grandparent Programs; American Association of Retired Persons (AARP), and Adult Basic Education programs.

ENDNOTES

1. Zimmerman, Bill. *How To Tape Instant Oral Biographies.* New York: Bantam Books, 1992.
2. Derman-Sparks, Louise. *Anti-Bias Curriculum: Tools for Empowering Young Children.* Washington, D.C.: National Association for the Education of Young Children, 1989. Also, McCracken, Janet Brown. *Valuing Diversity: The Primary Years.* Washington, D.C.: National Association for the Education of Young Children, 1993.

7 OUTREACH TO FAMILIES THROUGH EARLY CARE AND EDUCATIONAL FACILITIES

Often families that could benefit the most from the services of public libraries do not come to the library, for a variety of reasons: They do not realize what libraries have to offer; do not understand the importance of reading to children on a daily basis; lack the time to come to the library; have no transportation; fear overdue fines; fear their children will damage books; cannot read themselves; speak and/or read a limited amount of English; are not readers themselves; are physically or mentally unable to bring their family; have no permanent address and are unable to get a library card; or are only concerned with surviving on a daily basis. Their young children are the ones who suffer as a result. Because these young children could profit most from the resources of a public library, it is important that every librarian serving youth spends some time doing outreach. Outreach is unquestionably necessary, and what one must decide is the amount of time to be spent in outreach programs and the amount spent for programming done in-house.

Many librarians feel that they do not have time to do outreach due to the large number of programs they must do in the library. From infant to toddler to preschool storytimes, to programs for older children, to the basic library work of ordering and weeding out books, attending continuing-education activities, and keeping up with technology, most librarians feel overwhelmed. Yet programs offered in the library usually reach the same people over and over again, those who probably would come to the library with or without the basic programs. Often the families reached are those who know the importance of reading to young children, while others in the community are ignored.

We expect people to come to our library if they want our services. Some librarians try to do outreach by scheduling programs on the importance of reading to young children in the library. When only two or three caregivers attend, they are disappointed. They may feel that they have tried to reach a new audience, which evidently was not interested, so why try anymore? Only when librarians go out of the library building and meet families in their own neighborhoods will they have a chance of reaching those who need to hear their message the most.

Their are two basic ways to reach those families not already coming to the library. One is through outreach directly to these families in their neighborhoods. The other is through reaching teachers or early childhood caregivers who have contact with the young children in these families. To be realistic, regardless of librarians' efforts, some family caregivers will be unreachable for different reasons. Instead of writing off these children, or trying unsuccessfully to reach their family caregivers, librarians may be more effective to reach teachers or early childhood educators who also spend many hours with these young children. By convincing members of the child-care and education community of the importance of reading aloud daily, these children are not forgotten. Both methods of outreach will be discussed in this chapter.

REACHING FAMILIES OUTSIDE THE LIBRARY

There are various ways to reach families outside of the library. Following are just a few of the caregivers you can target and where to reach them. More information on outreach to some of these specific groups will be given in Chapter 8. You may also wish to consult *Managing Library Outreach Programs: A How-To-Do-It Manual for Librarians* by Marcia Trotta (Neal-Schuman, 1993).

1. Book giveaway programs to caregivers of new babies born in local hospitals,
2. Head Start parents at Parent Advisory Committee meetings,
3. Parents attending well-baby clinics,
4. Mothers attending WIC (Women, Infant, and Children) centers,
5. Caregivers visiting pediatrician's offices,
6. Child-development centers,
7. Family-health centers,
8. Families at homeless centers,

9. Families at battered women's centers,
10. Families at welfare centers,
11. Caregivers at food-stamp sites,
12. Teen parents at vocational or high schools,
13. Mothers in prison,
14. Families at migrant camps,
15. Families in housing projects or low-income housing,
16. Parent meetings at schools,
17. Meetings of home-schooled families,
18. Caregivers attending adult literacy classes, and
19. Foster-parent groups.

After targeting a group you want to reach, you must make contact with the organizations through which you will meet these caregivers. Explain what you have in mind and why you want to target the group. Tell in detail what you would like to say to the caregivers. You may get assistance from the organization or ideas of ways things should be done differently.

When meeting caregivers for the first time, keep it simple. Do not assume that they understand how a library operates or what resources you have. However, it is important not to talk down to caregivers. You will be respected more if you can keep a conversational tone and attempt to fit into the activity you are attending. For example, if you are attending a Head Start Parent Advisory Committee and they are making items for their children, you may just want to sit down and help and talk to the parents as you are working. When meeting this group a second time, demonstrate how to share books with their children. Make sure you have suggested book lists and age-appropriate language-activity sheets (finger plays, rhymes, songs) that will help them with literacy activities at home.

Establishing deposit-book collections in as many agencies as possible also may reach those families not already coming to the library. Ideal deposit collections provide library books on a regular basis and are changed frequently. Some libraries with limited funds provide paperback books or even discarded books still in usable condition.

In addition to or instead of deposit collections, other libraries have provided themed totes or kits that are dropped off at agencies that serve families. Each tote or kit usually contains books on a theme along with cassettes, games, puzzles, toys, or puppets, plus a literacy-related activity sheet.

Some libraries have received grant monies or funds from local organizations or businesses and have been able to provide book giveaway programs. This allows children to own some of their own books. If you provide this type of project, it is still important to convince these people of the benefits of using the public library to obtain more books for daily reading at home.

REACHING EARLY CHILDHOOD CAREGIVERS OR TEACHERS OF YOUNG CHILDREN

Many family caregivers of young children are unreachable, for whatever reason. Libraries should not forget these children, however. The way to reach them is through their teachers, whether they are preschool, Head Start, day-care, home-school or public-school teachers. These people often spend more time with the children than the family caregiver and can have a huge influence on their literacy growth.

The following statistics are from a National Center for Education Statistics survey that was taken in 1991:

1. "About 5.7 million (68 percent) preschool children nation-wide were receiving care or education from a relative or nonrelative in a home-based setting or in an organized non-residential group setting."[1]
2. "On average, preschoolers spend a total of 19 hours per week in care and education programs, with black children spending more hours per week than either white or Hispanic children, or children of other ethnic groups."[2]

In a report recording these statistics, the following was also noted: ". . . labor force participation rates of women with children three to five years old rose from 31.8 percent in 1970 to 54.8 percent in 1990 . . ."[3]

These telling statistics show that some young children may be reached easier through their public caregivers. Many public libraries have realized the importance of reaching these people and have made a more direct effort using a variety of methods. Following are some of the more common ways to reach these caregivers of young children through public-library outreach services:

Storytime Kits: Many libraries have compiled storytime kits that can be used by early childhood educators or caregivers. Some kits are theme-based, while others, which stay at centers for a longer period of time, contain a large number of developmentally appropriate materials. Kits often include picture books; early childhood resource books; musical cassettes; puppets or other realia; and activity sheets that contain songs, finger plays, and other language activities. Some also include public-performance videos, flannel-board sets, games, or toys. Kits are usually circulated in two ways: Early childhood educators pick up the kits at a library or agency, or kits are dropped off directly at the early childhood centers or home-care sites. The advantage of librarians and others dropping off kits is that they reach more people who probably would not make the effort to pick them up. For many caregivers, the convenience of having the kits delivered to their sites means they read to their children more often. Though some libraries have staff members drop off kits, others have volunteers, often senior citizens or members of Friends' groups, deliver kits. Another major advantage of kits is that early childhood centers often cannot afford to buy many books, and thus have few good books to read to the children or must read the same books over and over again. Unless they stop at a library frequently to borrow books, children often have few good books read to them on a regular basis. Numerous libraries across the nation are circulating storytime kits. Two different programs are highlighted here.

Sample Program: Project LEAP; Cuyahoga County Public Library, 2111 Snow Rd., Parma, OH 44134. Contact: Jan Smuda. LEAP stands for the Library's Educational Alternative for Preschoolers. Originally funded by LSCA grants, the service is now completely funded by the library system. Thematic storytime kits circulate to day cares, nursery schools, and numerous other early childhood facilities. Kits are picked up by caregivers at local library locations. Over 1,000 kits are available. Each boxed kit contains eight books for various age levels but basically covering toddler to age five; a music cassette; an object or realia item; and an activity sheet. The program employs a full-time Early Childhood Specialist. Other components are circulating puppet kits; staff training; workshops by professional speakers; a newsletter; and a model core-book collection for early childhood centers.

Sample Program: Child Care/Library Outreach; NOLA Regional Library System, 4445 Mahoning Ave. N.W., Warren, OH 44483. Contact: author of this publication. NOLA is a regional library system encompassing 35 public-library and 42 school-district library systems in eight counties. Rather than kits being picked up at the library, participating public libraries have a children's librarian drop off a new storytime kit monthly at the center. The hope is that child-care providers who do not normally use the library, or that may have only a small collection of books at their center, will have easier access to books and materials to encourage more frequent literacy experiences. The desire is also to have children's librarians establish rapport with the child-care providers, enabling them to form a partnership to enhance preschoolers' literacy skills. Large Tupperware kits are sent through a delivery system from one library system to another at the end of the month. Kits contain 20 picture books; one big book; one resource book; a musical cassette; a literature-based public-performance video; and a puppet, floor puzzle, or other realia item. An annual workshop on sharing books, storytelling, literature extensions, and how to have a literacy-rich classroom is provided in each county for child-care providers and educators.

Bookmobiles or Vans Visiting Centers: Some libraries include early childhood centers or home day-care sites on their bookmobile runs or have vans that directly visit centers to drop off books. Bookmobiles allow children to come on board and pick out books themselves. Others allow caregivers to pick books for small deposit collections. If time and staffing permits, storytimes are sometimes conducted during these visits. Five sample programs are noted here.

Sample Program: King County Library System, 300 Eighth Ave. N., Seattle, WA 98109. Contact: Mary Kay Dahlgreen and Kathleen Sullivan. King County Library System has a children's outreach service that visits child care facilities for six week training sessions. A half-hour storytime is conducted and a sheet with stories, crafts, finger plays, and ways to extend storytimes is distributed. Theme kits are being developed for circulation.

Sample Program: Magic Bus; Denver Public Library, 1357 Broadway, Denver, CO 80203. Denver Public Library had a brightly decorated bus that visited preschools and child-care centers delivering books, storytimes, and craft ideas. Approximately 15 to 20 centers were visited weekly. (Discontinued—personal visits only.)

Sample Program: Read Rover; Baltimore County Public Library, 320 York Rd., Towson, MD 21204. Contact: Kathleen Reif. A decorated bookmobile called the Read Rover visits family day-care providers so that they can check out books, cassettes, videocassettes, and "programs-to-go" to use in their centers. Making 79 stops a month, the vehicle travels four days a week, 52 weeks a year. Age-appropriate storytimes and puppet shows are also conducted on the bookmobile. Brochures are given to children, urging parents to visit their closest library branch with their children.

Sample Program: West Hartford Public Library, 20 S. Main St., West Hartford, CT 06107. Contact: Carol Waxman. The West

Hartford Public Library provides day-care delivery service on a monthly basis to licensed daycare homes. A tote bag containing a dozen picture books and several educational activity books are delivered by a volunteer driver.

Sample Program: Project BEACON; The Carnegie Library of Pittsburgh, Homewood Branch, 7101 Hamilton Ave., Pittsburgh, PA 15208. This is one component of the very successful Beginning With Books Project described below under "Book Giveaway Programs." In Project BEACON, services are to children in day-care and public-housing settings. Storymobiles are stocked with children's books and other resource books on emergent literacy, child development, child care, and parenting. Community-outreach assistants work out of neighborhood branches of the library and visit more than 60 day-care sites every month and make bimonthly stops at public-housing projects. Storytimes are provided, caregivers are urged to read aloud daily, and visits to public libraries are encouraged.

Deposit Collections Housed at Child-Care Offices: Several libraries house a collection of books at county child-care offices or Head Start sites. Teachers can check out books and then take them back to their centers. Some just use the books in the centers, while others allow the children to take the books home for family members to read. This often resolves the problem of parents getting to the library with their children.

Sample Program: Lee County Library System, 2050 Lee St., Fort Myers, FL 33901. A home circulating library is housed in the Lee County Child Care Offices. Teachers check out books every other week to take back to their centers and children in turn are allowed to take books home. 100 thematic book activity kits are also distributed.

Newsletters: Various libraries compile a newsletter specifically for early childhood caregivers. These publications often list new books, including resource books, and suggest various learning activities such as crafts, recipes, songs, and other literature extensions. Upcoming programs offered by the library are advertised. Newsletters can also be one- or two-page masters that can be reproduced by centers and sent home with children for distribution to parents.

Sample Program: Baltimore County Public Library, 320 York Rd., Towson, MD 21204. Contact: Lynne Degen. *Day by Day: Feasts and Frolics for Day Care Providers* is a bimonthly newsletter sent to licensed in-home day-care providers. In addition to ideas on sharing children's books, simple projects from books contained in the library's collection are cited along with riddles and puzzles for children. Library and agency programs, workshops, and day-care certification courses are noted.

Book Giveaway Programs: Libraries that have funding provided through grants, local organizations, or corporations, may distribute free books through preschool centers, day-care sites, health agencies or other child-care agencies or public-housing sites.

Sample Program: Beginning With Books; The Carnegie Library of Pittsburgh, Homewood Branch, 7101 Hamilton Ave., Pittsburgh, PA 15208. Contact: Joan Brest Friedberg and Elizabeth Segel. There are numerous components to this extensive program for disadvantaged families with preschool children, including the Gift Book Program, The Read Aloud Parents Club, and the Read Together Program. The one featured here is the gift-book program. Packets of paperback or board books (each packet contains three books of the highest literary quality) are given away to families through social-service agencies, day cares, and nurseries. A booklet with information on reading aloud and lists of local library programs are included. Each family also hears from a member of the staff or a cooperating agency about the importance of daily family reading. Funding is from private foundations, federal government money, and local contributors. The Carnegie Library contributes salary support and in-kind services and publishers offer books at 50 to 60 percent discounts. (See also Project BEACON above.)

Sample Program: Babywise; Youth Services Dept., Nassau Library System, 900 Jerusalem Ave., Uniondale, NY. Contact: Caroline Ward. Library staff first contact Head Start directors, then schedule a time to speak at Head Start Parents' meetings. A talk on the importance of reading aloud and sharing books is given. A silver tote bag is given to each parent with a copy of Good Night Moon, a brochure on reading aloud, a pamphlet about library programs and materials, and a coupon for a second free book to be picked up at the library. Funding was through a three year LSCA grant.

Model Storytimes: Librarians may visit centers to model to early childhood educators how to do storytimes. The hope is that early childhood caregivers will become comfortable reading to children and sharing language activities and realize how important it is to share such activities on a daily basis. If library staffing does not permit this, librarians may train volunteers in storytime skills and these volunteers can in turn provide storytimes when furnishing kits to early childhood caregivers.

Sample Program: Sharing the Gift; Harford County Library, 1221-A Brass Mill Rd., Bel Air, MD 21017. Volunteers are recruited that are willing to share the joy of picture books with young children in preschool centers. Library staff train these volunteers in storytelling and the use of music, finger plays, and audiovisual materials. Each trained volunteer is requested to provide a minimum of a half-day each month for six months to introduce literature-based programs to children in preschools. The actual programs used including books, filmstrips, puppets, poems, and dramatic activities are prepared for the volunteers by the children's librarians.

Resource Collections: Many libraries have set up special parent and teacher sections in their libraries with resource books that will be useful to caregivers of young children. Sending flyers to centers advertising these sections and listing materials available may encourage more caregivers to use library resources. Books that would be useful as resource books for early childhood educators are listed in Chapter 4 under "Resources for Librarians Who Serve Young Children." Other books, specifically geared to early childhood teachers, and that are developmentally appropriate for young children, are often more difficult to find. These books are not normally reviewed in library literature and are from smaller presses or presses that publish early childhood materials. Some catalogs to check for these books are from the following publishers: *The National Association for the Education of Young Children, Gryphon House, Building Blocks,* and *Totline.* A listing of useful books for early childhood educators and the addresses for the above publishers follows (see Fig. 7.1).

Workshops: A very basic program that all librarians can provide easily and with no additional funding, is workshops for early childhood educators. These should be offered during evening hours or on Saturdays, for obvious reasons. You also can contact your local chapter of The National Association for the Education of Young Children and volunteer to provide a workshop. The importance

---

FIGURE 7.1 Resource Books for Early Childhood Educatiors (in addition to those listed in Chapter4)

Bond, Carol. *Marmalade Days: Fall.* Also, *Winter* and *Spring.* Mt. Rainier, Md.: Gryphon House, 1987.

Bredekamp, Susan, Ed. *Developmentally Appropriate Practice in Early Childhood Programs Serving Children From Birth Through Age 8.* Expanded Ed. Washington, D.C.: National Association for the Education of Young Children, 1987.

Brown, Sam, Ed. *Bubbles, Rainbows and Worms: Science Activities for Young Children.* Mt. Rainier, Md.: Gryphon House, 1981.

Brown, Sam, Ed. *One, Two, Buckle My Shoe: Math Activities for Young Children.* Mt. Rainier, Md.: Gryphon House, 1981.

Carlson, Laurie. *EcoArt!: Earth-Friendly Art and Craft Experiences for 3-to 9-Year-Olds.* Charlotte, Vt.: Williamson, 1993.

Derman-Sparks, Louise and the A.B.C. Task Force. *Anti-Bias Curriculum: Tools for Empowering Young Children.* Washington, D.C.: National Association for the Education of Young Children, 1989.

Frank, Marjorie. *I Can Make a Rainbow.* Nashville, Tenn.: Incentive Publications Inc., 1976.

Herr, Judy A. and Yvonne K. Libby. *Creative Resources for the Early Childhood Classroom.* Albany: Delmar, 1990.

Indenbaum, Valerie. *Everything Book.* Livonia, Mich.: Partner Press, 1983.

Johnson, Barbara, and Betty Plemons. *Cup Cooking: Individual Child Portion Picture Recipes.* Ithaca, N.Y.: Early Educator's Press, 1990.

Kohl, Mary Ann, and Jean Potter. *Science Arts: Discovering Science Through Art Experiences.* Bellingham, Wash.: Bright Ring, 1993.

Miller, Karen. *Ages and Stages.* Owings Mills, Md.: Telshare, 1985.

Miller, Karen. *The Outside Play and Learning Book.* Mt. Rainier, Md.: Gryphon House, 1989.

Milord, Susan. *The Kids' Nature Book.* Charlotte, Vt.: Williamson, 1989.

Milord, Susan. *Hands Around the World: 365 Ways to Build Cultural Awareness and Global Respect.* Charlotte, Vt.: Williamson, 1992.

Mitchell, Dr. Grace. *A Very Practical Guide to Discipline.* Owings Mills, Md.: Telshare, 1982.

Newmann, Dana. *Early Childhood Teacher's Almanack: Activities for Every Month of the Year.* West Nyack, N.Y.:Center for Applied Research in Education, 1984.

Petrash, Carol. *Earthways.* Mt. Rainier, MD.: Gryphon House, 1992.

Rockwell, Robert E., Elizabeth A. Sherwood, and Robert A. Williams. *Hug a Tree and Other Things to Do Outdoors With Young Children.* Mt. Rainier, Md.: Gryphon House, 1983.

Sanford, Anne R., et al. *Planning Guide to the Preschool Curriculum.* Revised Ed. Lewisville, N.C.: Kaplan, 1983.
Schiller, Pam, and Joan Rossano. *The Instant Curriculum.* Mt. Rainier, Md.: Gryphon House, 1990.

Shea, Jan Fisher. *No Bored Babies: A Guide to Making Developmental Toys for Babies Birth—Age Two.* Seattle, Wash.: Bear Creek, 1986.

Sherwood, Elizabeth, Robert A. Williams, and Robert E. Rockwell. *More Mudpies to Magnets: Science for Young Children.* Mt. Rainier, Md.: Gryphon House, 1990. Also, *Mudpies to Magnets.*

Smith, Charles. *The Peaceful Classroom: One Hundred Sixty-Two Easy Activities to Teach Preschoolers Compassion and Cooperation.* Mt. Rainier, Md.: Gryphon House, 1993.

FIGURE 7.1 Continued

Stassevitch, Verna, and others. *Ready-to-Use Activities for Before and After School Programs.* West Nyack, N.Y.: Center for Applied Research in Education, 1989.

Stavros, Sally, and Lois Peters. *Big Learning for Little Learners.* Livonia, Mich.: Partner Press, 1987.

York, Stacey. *Roots and Wings: Affirming Culture in Early Childhood Settings.* St. Paul, Minn.: Redleaf, 1991.

Addresses for Catalogs

Building Blocks
38W567 Brindlewood
Elgin, IL 60123

National Association for the Education of Young Children
1509 16th Street N.W.
Washington, D.C. 20036-1426

Gryphon House
Early Childhood Teacher Books
P.O. Box 275
Mt. Rainier, MD 20712

Totline Press
Warren Publishing House
P.O. Box 2250
Everett, WA 98203

---

of reading to young children, how to read to young children, good books to share, and ways to share books and incorporate literature extensions such as music, finger plays, creative dramatics, and other learning activities can be discussed. Multiple copies of resource books and picture books that are shared should be purchased so educators can check out materials later at the library. To advertise such a program, check telephone yellow pages listing public, private, religious-affiliated, or employer-based early childhood centers, day cares, and preschools; contact Head Start agencies; consult the local day-care licensing office for a list of local day-care homes; and notify vocational schools, colleges, and public and private schools that teach early childhood classes. An excellent resource book with sample lectures that can be presented to different groups is *First Steps to Literacy: Library Programs for Parents, Teachers, and Caregivers* edited by Nell Colburn and Maralita Freeny and prepared by the Preschool Services and Parent Education Committee for the Association for Library Service to Children of the American Library Association (1990). Following is a sample outline of a workshop that can be offered to early childhood caregivers (see Fig. 7.2). It should be tailored to fit the group in attendance.

Libraries should have a list of preschools, Head Start centers, licensed day cares, and schools in their service districts. A check of the telephone directory will provide most of the needed information. Most private, public, and religious-affiliated centers are

FIGURE 7.2 Sample Topics to be Included In a Workshop For Early Childhood Educators

  I. Why Share Literature With Young Children
    A. Importance of Sharing Books and Language Activities from Birth
    B. Importance of Sharing Books on a Daily Basis
    C. Literacy Rates/Statistics
    D. Importance of Learning in the Early Years
    E. Effects of Television/Videos
    F. Caregivers as Models and the Importance of Their Reading Habits
    G. Role Early Childhood Educators Can Play in Young Children's Literacy Skills
 II. Sharing Books With Young Children—How To's
    A. How to Pick Good Books to Read and That You Enjoy
    B. Picking Books Considering Young Children's Developmental Stages
    C. Suggested Guides or Resource Books for Selection & Using Librarians for Suggestions
    D. What to Look For When Selecting Books
    E. What Children Are Learning When You Read to Them
    F. The Importance of Picture Book Art
    G. Types of Books to Avoid
    H. How to Read Books
       1. How to Hold Books
       2. Reading with Enthusiasm/Using Different Voices
       3. How to Talk About Books after Sharing Them
    I. Special Types of Books/Materials to Share in Addition to Picture Books
       1. Board and Cloth Books for Very Young Children
       2. Folk/Fairy Tales
       3. Wordless Books
       4. Informational Books
       5. Concept Books
       6. Audiotapes/Musical Cassettes/Videos Etc.
III. Methods of Storytelling
    A. Participation Stories
    B. Creative Dramatics
    C. Flannel Board/Magnetic Board/Velcro Board
    D. Tell & Draw Stories
    E. Clothesline Stories
    F. String Stories
    G. Puppetry
    H. Use of Props
 IV. Literature Extensions
    A. Art Extensions
    B. Music Extensions
    C. Mother Goose/Poetry/Rhyme/Rap/Fingerplays
    D. Science Extensions
    E. Math Extensions
    F. Cooking Extensions
    G. Nature Extensions

FIGURE 2.1 Continued

V. How to Set Up a Literacy-Rich Classroom
    A. Book Area
    B. Creative Dramatics Area
    C. Puppet Area
    D. Writing Center
    E. Other Areas—Music etc.
VI. Do's to Promote Literacy Experiences
    A. Read Aloud to Children on a Daily Basis
    B. Read to Children for Enjoyment—Not to Teach Them to Read or to Learn Phonics
    C. Do Not Use Worksheets, Ditto Sheets or Coloring Sheets
    D. Allow Children to Ask Questions About Books You Have Read
    E. Talk About the Books You Have Read
    F. Read Different Types of Stories
    G. Use Wordless Books and Have Children Tell the Story Through the Pictures
    H. Use Literature Extensions Whenever Possible
    I. Have a Variety of Writing Materials
    J. Have Books For Children to Look at During Free Times

---

listed. One should also remember employer-provided care centers and public and private schools with preschool programs. Data on licensed day cares and homeschooled students in your area takes more effort however. Because both must be licensed, a check with licensing agents at a regional or state level can provide this information. Information on unlicensed home-care sites is much more difficult to obtain. Try checking newspaper classified ads and bulletin boards located at supermarkets, local churches, or laundromats.

Librarians should stay active in their local chapter of the National Association for the Education of Young Children. Most of these chapters have annual workshops or meetings where librarians can present new picture books and/or offer ideas for storytelling, easy puppets, finger plays, and other literature extensions.

ENDNOTES

1. U.S. Department of Education, Office of Educational Research and Improvement. Profile of Preschool Children's Child Care and Early Education Program Participation. (Washington, D.C.: GPO, 1993), p. v.
2. Ibid., p. v.
3. Ibid., p. 3.

8 OUTREACH TO FAMILIES OF SPECIAL POPULATIONS

The previous chapter discussed the importance of reaching families not already coming to the library. A listing of places to reach families was noted. In this chapter, several of those special populations will be mentioned in more detail, with suggestions as to how to serve these families. Sample programs that are or were working successfully in a public library are given. These special populations include families with children who have special needs; bilingual families or those in which English is the second language; families that reside in housing projects or migrant camps/housing; those that reside in centers such as homeless centers or domestic-violence crisis centers; families that are separated, with the mothers in correctional facilities or children in hospitals, shelters, or institutions; and those that need extra guidance, mainly teen parents.

No library can be all things to all people in a community. It would be difficult for any library system, regardless of size and staffing, to be able to provide all the outreach necessary to serve all the groups listed above. Begin by targeting one group that you feel needs the resources of the library the most and which may not be attending literacy programs elsewhere in the community. What group in the community is really being ignored by the library? Are you duplicating the efforts of others such as schools, literacy groups, or organizations in the area? What families could benefit from the library's resources that are simply not being served now?

FAMILIES WITH CHILDREN WHO HAVE SPECIAL NEEDS

How does one define a child who has "special needs"? In a book written for the National Association for the Education of Young Children, author Phyllis Chandler defines a child as having special needs if "he or she is in some way outside the range of what we consider to be characteristic of a particular age . . . although each child is unique and children naturally differ from one another, the child with special needs differs from the average child in some way beyond that found in the normal range of individual differences."[1] These differences may be in the area of physical, mental, social, or emotional development, and children may have more than one disability.

Public Law 94-142 requires that all handicapped children have available to them a free appropriate public education in the least-restrictive educational environment. Least restrictive does not necessarily mean a regular classroom, but children with special needs do have more opportunities to be in a regular classroom than in the past. Today, many children with special needs are included in normal early childhood programs with children who are not classified as special-needs children. This inclusion is recommended by educators for a number of reasons: Children with special needs learn developmentally appropriate behavior easier if included with typical children who are good role models; more realistic expectations will be placed on special-needs children if they are included with children with more typical behaviors, and expectations often determine how children behave; they will be more readily accepted by other children because they are not isolated; and all children will react more positively toward those with special needs when accepted by their peers due to their own individual strengths.[2]

Because of the Americans with Disabilities Act, which went into effect in 1992, librarians also need to be able to accommodate children with special needs in all programs offered at the public library. All public facilities must be accessible and programs should be open and available to all children, typical or with special needs. Sometimes room arrangements must be changed or materials used in programs must be substituted to accommodate individual children. Most libraries will include a statement on program flyers that, if children require special services, the library should be notified in advance. For information on programming in the library setting with children with special needs, consult the ALSC Program Support Publication *Programming for Serving Children With Special Needs,*[3] *The Preschooler and the Library* by Ann D. Carlson,[4] and *Serving the Disabled,* a Neal-Schuman publication.[5]

More often, however, children with special needs are not regularly attending library programs and thus librarians should consider some type of outreach to these children. This requires cooperation not only with agencies that serve these children, but also with the family.

Many librarians are uncomfortable planning programs for children with special needs because they feel that they have had no special training in this area. Yet these children are no different from other children and are capable of learning, though it may be in a different way. All children benefit from the exposure to daily reading aloud. One only needs to read Dorothy Butler's moving account of her severely disabled granddaughter in *Cushla and Her Books* to be assured of this fact. The most notable accomplishment of Cushla's parents was their constant positive attitude and that they believed that reading books to Cushla would make a difference. This was evident in both her language and cognitive abilities. Librarians can profit from this experience by having a positive attitude about the children they are serving. Realizing that the sharing of books is possible and necessary should ease feelings of discomfort.

There are various organizations you may contact when locating special-needs children in your community. Check yellow pages phone listings for Easter Seal Societies, child-learning or development centers, programs for developmental delays, human-service agencies, social-service organizations, rehabilitation services, hearing and speech centers, mental-health centers, community health centers, behavioral-health centers, societies for the blind, etc.

When contacting an agency you intend to work with, find out as much about the children and their families as possible. By receiving this specific information, you may research ahead of time any disability or condition that you do not understand. Focus on the children's capabilities, rather than what they are incapable of doing. Then choose materials to share that you feel will meet these families' needs. Often materials will be no different than those you use with typical children, though there may be some differences, such as books for children that have only partial sight. As a rule, family caregivers of young children with special needs are more involved in their children's education by necessity, so allow time for family caregivers to tell you about their children and listen carefully. It may help you to suggest other books or materials that will be useful to their particular family.

When doing a program at an agency, ask the coordinators for their support and help. Explain to them what you are planning to do. Do they have any other suggestions, or do they feel you should be doing something differently? Because they have had contact with the families and their children, they will be able to assist you in many ways, including supplying information such as where the children are developmentally. They will also be able to provide special help where needed. For example, if children are deaf or hearing impaired, and you are using stories, songs, and finger plays and do not know sign language, make sure that you have shared materials ahead of time with the person who will sign the program.

In most programs for children with special needs, you may want to include more flannel-board or visual stories, repetitive stories, realia, creative dramatics, music, puppetry, films, or videos, depending on the capabilities of your audience. Some children learn better through one means than another, and agency coordinators will know which modes are more consistent with children's learning styles. By discussing this in advance, you may discover what activities would be enjoyed or appreciated the most, and how you need to adapt these for your audience. You will also be aware of what special materials you need to take with you. Libraries should own some examples of these specific materials for children with special needs and know how more can be obtained. These may include items such as special equipment; books in Braille or books that combine print and Braille; large-print books; special computer software; signed videos; descriptive videos; audio-book tapes; talking books; tactile books; movable books; and books about children with special needs so that these children can identify with others in similar circumstances.

The most important thing you can do is be accepting of children with special needs and relate to them as you would any other child you serve. Remember that they will benefit if family caregivers read to them and share language on a daily basis, and it is your goal to provide materials and convince caregivers of this. You need to explain how all library programs are open to their children and that you would like to accommodate them in any programs they would desire to attend at the library. Finally, remember to think positively when you are working with families who have children with special needs. Your positive feelings and enthusiasm can translate to the whole family so that they know sharing books and language makes a difference.

Sample Program: Brooklyn Public Library, Brooklyn, NY 11238. Brooklyn Public Library has a "Child's Place for Children with Special Needs" established at its Flatlands Branch Library. The location is wheelchair accessible and equipped with special furniture, toys, and appropriate books. Books and reference materials for adult caregivers are also included. The center is equipped to handle children from ages birth through nine years and their families, caregivers, and educators. Funding is from the New York State Department of Education. Special programs held in the library include storytimes held after school and toys for tots, designed to involve the entire family in the use of educational toys. An outreach component that can be modeled by other libraries is also included. Class visits are made to schools that serve disabled children. Each visit is different, designed to accommodate the disabilities of the children involved.

OUTREACH TO BILINGUAL FAMILIES

The United States has seen an increase in the number of immigrant and refugee families over the last decade. Therefore it is much more likely to have families in the library's service area that have a native language other than English, and in some communities, it is commonplace. According to a report released by the National Center for Education Statistics, between 1979 and 1989, the number of people reported to speak a language other than English at home increased by about 40 percent. This figure continues to rise rapidly.[6] U.S. Census Bureau statistics from 1990 indicate that 14 percent of the nation's population speaks a language other than English at home (compared to 11 percent in 1980). The top languages spoken include (in millions of speakers): Spanish, 17.4; French, 1.7; German, 1.6; Italian, 1.3; Chinese, 1.3; Tagalog (language of the Philippines), .84; Polish, .72; Korean, .63; Vietnamese, .51; and Portuguese, .43.[7]

Ethnic pride and heritage are positive aspects of our society today, and preserving a family's native language is just as important as learning English as a second language. In some families, caregivers only know their native language and not English. Even if the children learn English in school, they must communicate in their native language at home. If family caregivers are unable to read books in English, and if the library does not have materials in other languages, children will miss out on a parent reading aloud to them on a daily basis. It is important that the library recognizes various cultural groups' rights to know and value their native language and heritage.

The federal government has established a Public Law, called the Bilingual Education Act, which declares " . . . it to be the policy of the United States, in order to establish equal educational opportunity for all children and to promote educational excellence . . . to encourage the establishment and operation, where appropriate, of educational programs using bilingual education practices, techniques, and methods . . . "[8] Public libraries have an obligation to provide programming with bilingual interpreters, to have materials for young children in different languages, or to own bilingual books.

When attempting outreach to bilingual families, it is important to be knowledgeable and sensitive to the various cultures and customs of those you are trying to contact. It is also vital to either be able to speak the language of the families or have an interpreter accompany you. You will want to share what the library has to offer. If speaking to a Spanish population, you may wish to distribute copies of *Helping Your Child Use the Library (Como ayudar a sus hijos a usar la biblioteca)*, available from the U.S. Department of Education, Library Programs, Office of Educational Research and Improvement (202-219-2293). Bilingual materials owned by the library should be displayed and some stories should be read or told. In addition to books, songs and finger plays in native languages should be shared. As mentioned previously, it is important to go to the family's neighborhood. The library will appear to be a more welcoming institution if bilingual programs and materials are provided. Remember though, that once inexperienced families come to the library, the facility and its new technology may seem overwhelming. Many families may be unwilling or unable to ask for help. It is crucial that there are staff members who can speak their language fluently or have at least a basic conversational knowledge of the language to help these patrons.

Where does one reach bilingual families? A good place to begin is through ethnic/cultural centers in the city, neighborhood churches, and ethnic organizations. Many of these organizations have newsletters. Advertise on radio stations that broadcast in languages other than English and place articles in native-language newspapers. Are there any English-as-Second-Language classes in your community? Are there English-as-Second Language summer-school classes for children? How about migrant workers' children's programs? Try to talk to these caregivers. Provide bilingual bibliographies and flyers concerning the library's materials and programs. Talk with the families about what the library has to offer, and what bilingual or native language materials the library owns. Do not forget to mention other formats such as *Living Books* on CD-ROM that contain text in at least three languages. Ask families for suggestions of other types of materials they would like to see. You may wish to plan library ethnic celebrations or programs in tandem with other cultural organizations and spread the word of the importance of the library at these functions.

Where does one find native-language or bilingual materials? Publishers are producing more bilingual books and foreign language books. A check of the major publishers' catalogs will supply information on these. It is also crucial to check with smaller presses that specialize in bilingual and native-language materials. *The Literary Market Place* or *American Book Trade Directory* should be helpful. Major review journals such as *Booklist* and *School Library Journal* regularly review books published in other languages. In addition, R.R. Bowker has produced *Spanish Books in Print (Libros En Ventana En Hispanoamerica Y Expana Plus)* on CD-ROM. *Global Books in Print* on CD-ROM was initiated in the fall of 1994. Ask the community you are serving if they can suggest titles or authors from their ethnic or racial group, or types of materials they would like to see in the library.

Following is just a sampling of recommended picture books for young children that are suitable for family sharing:

> Bozylinsky, Hannah Heritage. *Lala Salama*. New York: Putnam & Grosset, 1993.
> Burstein, Fred. *The Dancer*. New York: Bradbury, 1993.
> Dorros, Arthur. *Radio Man*. New York: HarperCollins, 1993.
> Emberley, Rebecca. *Let's Go: A Book in Two Languages*. Boston: Little, Brown, 1993. Emberley,
> Rebecca. *My Day: A Book in Two Languages*. Boston: Little, Brown, 1993.
> Emberley, Rebecca. *My House = Mi Casa: A Book in Two Languages*. Boston: Little, Brown, 1990.
> Reiser, Lynn. *Margaret and Margarita, Margarita y Margaret*. New York: Greenwillow, 1993.
> Torres, Leyla. *Subway Sparrow*. New York: Farrar Straus Giroux, 1993.

Sample Program: Begin at the Beginning With Books; County of Los Angeles Public Library, 7400 E. Imperial Highway, Downey, CA 90241. Contact: Penny Markey, Coordinator of Youth Services. This bilingual outreach program attempts to reach pregnant women before their babies' births. There are three basic components to the program: to encourage mothers to use songs, stories, and nursery rhymes with their children; to inform the family of library resources; and to present parenting skills, including educational, health, nutrition, and parenting issues. Mothers are reached by bilingual librarians at selected county prenatal health clinics during their regularly scheduled appointments. Families who use the health clinics are multi-ethnic and earn $12,000 or less a year. Each time mothers attend the BBB presentations, they receive a small gift such as safety plugs, medicine spoons, little puppets, doorknob holders, or bookmarks etc. Most mothers have toddlers accompanying them, and informal storytimes are held. When the babies are born, mothers receive a card congratulating them on their new baby. In addition, they are asked to show a library card or apply for one to redeem a coupon for a teddy bear. Baby reunions are held monthly in participating libraries. Infant and toddler storytimes are held simultaneously for more modeling experiences for the caregivers. Incentive gifts are given, such as Polaroid pictures, books, etc. Families receive a certificate of participation after one year. The success of the program is due to the development of an on-going educational process and the personal relationship between the program staff and the new mothers and their babies.

OUTREACH TO FAMILIES THAT RESIDE IN CENTERS

Families that are residing temporarily in centers—such as homeless centers, domestic-violence crisis centers, welfare hotels, or other types of transient shelters—are obviously overwhelmed, simply trying to meet their everyday needs. However one of these basic needs is the education of their children. Because reading to young children is vital for their future education, it is important that these families share books with their young children. However, many of these caregivers do not realize the importance of daily reading to their child's future education. They often think that children do not learn to read until they enter school, so it is not necessary to read to them before then. Many feel that books are for children who already know how to read. Others have limited literacy skills. Because their lives are so stressful, reading to their children does not seem like a priority. Getting the message across on the importance of daily reading aloud and sharing language with children from birth is crucial for these caregivers.

Reading aloud is beneficial to young children in centers for reasons other than their future success in school or educational abilities. It also allows families to share time together, to be close, to escape from daily problems, and to calm children's fears and anger. Books can be used as bibliotherapy to present subjects that may have caused anguish or hurt to children, such as a sense of loss or separation, moving anxiety, family dissensions, and physical or sexual abuse.

Just how common is it to find families residing in centers? Looking at just one type—homeless families—should give an idea. In 1993, estimates by the Children's Defense Fund placed the proportion of the homeless population that are families with children at 36 percent. An estimated 100,000 children are homeless each night.[9]

Unfortunately for those residing in centers, libraries do not necessarily have a positive image. For caregivers with limited literacy skills, a library can be a very threatening institution. Having low self-esteem due to family situations or living arrangements does not make an educational institution a desirable place to go for help. Some libraries require forms of identification showing a permanent address to apply for a library card. The San Francisco Public Library addressed this problem by allowing homeless people to register with participating social-service providers. These providers issue statements on their agency letterhead that these homeless individuals are in contact with them, that they reside in San Francisco, and, if necessary, can use the agency's address for mail service.[10]

Some public libraries have tried extending service to these families by creating "lending libraries" or book deposits in centers. The selection of books for these lending libraries is very important. The collection should be balanced between information-providing or subject-oriented books, and picture books, common folk tales, and books for infants and toddlers. Parenting books, and musical and book cassettes with cassette players, should be provided if possible. Wordless books should also be included for those caregivers who cannot read, so that they can "tell the story" through the pictures. Books selected should depict families or situations that children in centers can relate to, and should reflect diverse ethnic groups and lifestyles.

Many of these libraries also have story programs for the families. Homeless children or children in centers often display problem behaviors such as short attention spans, speech and language delays, aggression, and withdrawal. Storytimes need to be tailored accordingly. Sharing finger plays, rhymes, and songs along with short, uncomplicated texts are important, as are participatory stories. Opportunities for the children to act out stories or be involved in body movements are also beneficial. Librarians should also talk to the caregivers about the importance of sharing literature and language, and demonstrate reading aloud and telling stories to the children. If possible, provide gift books that families can keep. Gift books are often donated—particularly to the homeless—by publishers, local organizations or individuals, or through Reading Is Fundamental's Project Open Book.

While it might not appear difficult to get families in centers to share books with their young children, it is actually rather challenging. There is usually a lack of knowledge on the importance of daily shared reading, as mentioned earlier, and many caregivers also are concerned that their children will damage books and they will need to pay for them. Family caregivers who are willing to share books may ask for books that are more educational—counting, alphabet, and skills-oriented books—rather than just read to their children for enjoyment. These are a few issues that librarians need to address when talking to these families.

Sample Program: Project Horizons. DeKalb County Public Library, 215 Syacamore Street, Decatur, GA 30030. Contact: Sherry Des Enfants. Children aged two to 13 years that live in eight homeless shelters in the county are reached at least once a week through this program, which has been in operation since 1989. Stories are told and caregivers are informally trained in read-aloud techniques and the importance of reading aloud. Deposit collections of both children's and adult donated paperback books are left in each shelter. These become the property of the residents and are not returned to the library. Materials are checked weekly, however, and rotated and replaced as needed. Four of the shelters received computers and personal software. Most of the books for the deposit collections are provided through RIF's Project Open Door. In addition, schools, businesses, churches, civic organizations, and private citizens have contributed books, magazines, and computer hardware and software. Over 50 volunteers work with four paid part-time storytellers reading, listening to children read, and helping with homework.

FAMILIES THAT RESIDE IN HOUSING PROJECTS OR MIGRANT CAMPS/HOUSING

Much of the detail given above for outreach to bilingual families and families that reside in centers applies to families that reside in low-income housing projects or in migrant camps/housing. Also, the information given in Chapter 3 on families that live in poverty and on family-literacy programs is applicable here. In this section, ideas on how to reach these families will be given along with a sample program.

Children living in conditions of poverty are all too prevalent in this country. According to statistics released by the Children's Defense Fund, 14.6 million children lived in poverty in 1992.[11] Many of these children are either homeless, living in welfare hotels, squalid rural shacks, migrant housing or camps, or in inner-city housing projects. The chances of these children owning books or having daily reading experiences are very slim. This does not of course preclude them from having literacy experiences, as stated in Chapter 3. In fact, while doing research for Kent State University, this author found that the best literacy experiences of any Head Start family interviewed, was the family that lived in the worst, most dangerous housing project.[12]

Connected with the problem of poverty is that normally family members living in these less than desirable situations also have low literacy skills. However, even these caregivers can be influenced to lay the foundation for their children's interest in language and books. They can learn from librarians who model telling stories and reading aloud, encouraging caregivers to continue the experience. They can also be taught to share word games, songs, and physical games. Many do not avail themselves of the services of a public library for various reasons, such as a lack of transportation and a lack of money to use public transportation to get to the library. These families often have not used the public library for most of their lives, and to try to convince them of a need for using it can be difficult.

As in other outreach services, it is vital to take the library to the people first. Many libraries visit sites with their bookmobiles, or house a small collection of books and materials at the outreach site. Some library systems have successfully supervised these on-site collections by having residents act as managers of the collection. With some basic training by librarians, these managers, instilled with pride, obtain the desire to help their fellow residents. Usually no fines are charged, due to people's inability to pay. Because of the pride so many feel in their library collections, theft and damage rates are usually low.

Other libraries have tried different approaches. The Chicago Public Library set up literacy initiative sites with computers for children at their housing authorities. Many of these children have little access to high technology, which often puts them further behind in school. The Peoria Public Library holds storytimes for children at housing projects where they play on street corners or near small on-site playgrounds. They also conduct individual apartment-to-apartment contacts. If funds allow, some libraries stock comic books, games, puzzles, audiovisual materials, and other manipulatives, because many of these children have few educational toys. Bookmobiles to migrant housing or camps have provided bilingual materials and bilingual storytimes.

Reaching low-income families is one mission that every public library can undertake, because almost every library has impoverished families in its community or service area.

Sample Program: Family Magic; Rockford Public Library, Rockford, IL. Contact: Estelle Black and Marcia Cook. This program targets parents and their children, ages three to five, who live in Rockford Housing Authority homes. Among program goals are those specific to library usage: to instill an interest in reading, to teach parents and children how to use the library, and to inform parents about the various adult-education opportunities available to them. There are 32 sessions in the series, 10 of which already involve library participation. Five programs in the series, each beginning with a storytime. Topics include using books at home; I am unique; this is my family; these are my feelings; and these are my fears. A book is given away at each session so that the family can begin a home library. Books include *A Boy, a Dog, and a Frog; Here Are My Hands; There's Something in My Attic; Grandpa's Face;* and *Alexander and the Terrible, Horrible, No Good, Very Bad Day.* The next five programs are held at the public library. The first meeting stresses the importance of reading, and stories are told by staff for parents and children. An extensive tour of the youth-services area is given at the second meeting, and parents are shown how to get library cards and check out books. The third session consists of a tour of the rest of the library for parents while children are entertained. On the fourth visit, parents meet with representatives of various educational institutions, while children enjoy a storytime. At the final meeting, parents talk to professionals about reliable child care and how to make their homes more "child safe," while children again enjoy a storytime. One book is given away at the end of each session so that families attending all sessions now own ten titles for their home library. The last five books include: *Ashanti to Zulu; Check It Out; Snowy Day; All the Colors of the Race;* and *The People Could Fly.* Because 90 percent of the participants are usually African-American, books include several titles representing participants' ethnic heritage.

Sample Program: Service to Migrant Farm Workers; Jane Morgan Memorial Public Library, Cambria, WI. Contact: Jeanne

Radke. Three mini-libraries were established in places accessible to where migrant workers, who come to Cambria from Texas, live and work. The children attend twice-weekly story programs. The libraries are stocked with books, newspapers, and magazines for adults and children in English and Spanish. A computer was also purchased. Laubach Literacy provides tutors that teach English to children and adults on a one-on-one basis.

FAMILIES THAT ARE SEPARATED, WITH MOTHERS IN CORRECTIONAL FACILITIES OR CHILDREN IN HOSPITALS, SHELTERS, OR INSTITUTIONS

Some young children are separated from their families for a period of time through the imprisonment of their mother or father, or for reasons that require them to be separated due to health, physical or verbal abuse, or other situations requiring protective custody.

These children need to realize that the library is there to help them. Books and the importance of reading still must be impressed upon them, and they will appreciate the joy and escapism that story programs can bring to their lives.

These programs require much more effort to set up. Visiting mothers or pregnant women in correctional facilities will take some coordination with authorities who are willing to support the library's efforts. Visiting shelters that house children in protective custody also is a major undertaking, because these children rarely are permitted to have outside visitors without supervision. Outreach to hospitalized children is easier to set up, but no easier to carry out.

After determining what facility you wish to serve, the initial contact may need to be made by a library director to a prison warden, or a shelter or hospital administrator. Several meetings may be required to clarify what you can and cannot do, and what would be most beneficial to the young children of imprisoned mothers or to sheltered or hospitalized children. In a prison situation you may end up working with a librarian or educator. In hospitals, there is usually a person who coordinates activities for children. It will be necessary to set up security precautions and find out prison, shelter, or hospital policies and procedures to know what you can and cannot do. For example, there may be certain items that are not allowed in correctional facilities or in shelter settings. It is best to start small in these situations and build up your program as time, staff, and finances allow.

Some of the same services provided to homeless families apply to children in shelters or hospitals. Emphasis is on deposit collections and story programs. For more information on serving hospitalized children, see Marcella Anderson's *Books and Children in Pediatric Settings: A Guide for Caregivers and Librarians.*[13]

Service to mothers in correctional facilities is probably one of the more challenging types of outreach. Picture books that are written for young children to learn to read can be used with these moms, with the added benefit that they will later be able to read these to their children. The goal of the library is the same as stressed in other programs—to make the mothers reading models for their children. It is important not only for the mothers to read to their children, but to show their children that reading is important to them. Librarians can help inmates make audiotapes of themselves reading books so that the children will be able to use the tapes when separated from their mother. Children's books should be available on days that children are allowed to visit their mothers in correctional facilities, and the audiotapes can be given or mailed to the homes of the children.

Sample Program: Library Stars; Orange County Public Library, 1501 E. St. Andrew Pl., Santa Ana, CA 92705. Contact: Pam Carlson, Project Director. The Orangewood Children's Home is an intake center for children, ages infancy through 17, in need of care due to abuse or neglect. Since these children are in protective custody, they are unable to visit a library on their own. The library went to them, establishing a "mini-branch" on the grounds of the property. Books, storytimes, library-skills training, and the opportunity for independent reading is provided. The name of the program, STARS, is an acronym for storytelling, activities, and reading in shelters. Activities include such things as puppets, crafts, music, creative dramatics, reader's theater, 16mm films, and videocassettes. Each child also receives a gift book to take with them.

Sample Program: From Parent to Child; Prince George's County Memorial Library System, Fairmount Heights Branch Library, 5904 Kolb St., Fairmount Heights, MD 20743. Contact: Honore Francois. This program, originally funded by grant money, is now discontinued. The library has a full-service library in a coeducational correctional facility. A grant funded a special program for women held at the detention center that had both a literacy and parenting component. Primary sponsors included the Department of Corrections, Prince George's County Library System, The Cooperative Extension System, and the Literacy Council of Prince George's County. Each series of programs lasted six weeks. Mothers attended on an almost daily basis, but one day a week was devoted to project activities. The literacy component was two-pronged, with the first part devoted to mothers. After assessing their skills, one-on-one tutoring was provided along with computer assistance. Mothers learned how to read to their children in the second part, and were exposed to a variety of activities to develop reading-readiness skills. Most of the mothers were young, and some still remembered nursery rhymes and finger plays from childhood. In addition to tips on reading aloud, they also learned how to tell stories, and made flannel-board stories, puppets, and items from everyday supplies, which they gave or sent to their children. The children visited the last session and both the mothers and librarians performed a program for the children. Mothers were able to have physical contact with their children and the session was videotaped.

OUTREACH TO TEEN PARENTS

Teen parents are one of the easiest of the special groups to reach and can benefit greatly from library services. Teen parents can be reached through high schools or vocational schools (often there are special classes for teen parents), through welfare centers, health clinics, parenting classes, or WIC programs. Teen parents who live with their parents or extended families may be more difficult to locate, though their children often attend day-care programs or Head Start centers. Teen parents also can be found in the other centers and sites mentioned previously.

How prevalent are teen parents? The Children's Defense Fund states that the teen birth rate for 1991 was 62.1 births per 1,000 girls aged 15 to 19. The estimated number of teen pregnancies for the same year was 1.1 million. The percentage of teen births that were to unmarried girls was 68.8 percent.[14]

These teenage parents need information on child rearing and development. They often have not completed their own education and need help accomplishing that with the added responsibility of raising a child. And most will have no idea of the importance of sharing books, language, and music with their baby. They do not know the significance of talking, rocking, and playing with their baby.

In addition to the importance of sharing literature, this is one group that will benefit by learning how to do finger plays and make puppets and books for their children. Many teens are still children themselves and will enjoy this hands-on experience and the knowledge that they are making or doing something that will benefit their young child. They will feel a real sense of accomplishment knowing that they have something to show for their efforts.

Sample Program: Building Blocks to Literacy; DeKalb County Public Library, 215 Sycamore St., Decatur, GA 30030. Contact: Sherry Des Enfants, Youth Services Coordinator. This is a literacy program for low-literacy teenage mothers. The goal is to teach the mothers to read so that they can in turn read to their children and help them learn language-building activities. Intended for mothers with infants up to 18 months old, each session lasts for approximately one hour. A 45-minute "play with a purpose" segment introduces mothers and their children to ways to interact meaningfully with infant and toddler toys such as blocks, knobbed puzzles, gym tubes, and tumble balls. A 15-minute "linguistic" segment where a librarian models ways to share board books, movement games, songs, and nursery rhymes concludes the program. Resource lists of appropriate books, toys, and audiovisual materials are distributed to help teens extend the experiences at home with their children.

A FINAL WORD ON OUTREACH PROGRAMS

Outreach programs are often funded by grants or other special funds and are often not a part of the library's normal operating budget. This is unfortunate, because the library mission should be to serve all people in the community. Usually those that could most benefit from library services can only be reached by the library going to them. Programs occasionally become part of the library's budget after grant funding, but more often during times of tight budgets and staffing, they are dropped. Some of the outreach programs described in this chapter and the preceding one may no longer be in service as you are read this book. And yet, in this time of changing technologies, shrinking budgets, and new roles, libraries more than ever must justify their existence. Libraries must be active, not passive, agents of change. Family-literacy programs are more vital than ever, and there is an increased knowledge of the importance of early childhood education. At an institute held at the University of Texas at Austin in spring of 1994, attended by librarians, early childhood educators, state children's consultants, library educators, and well-known speakers in the field of library science and early childhood education, a prototype was established for libraries to model when attempting to meet the first National Education Goal that "all children in America will start school ready to learn by the year 2000." In this prototype, libraries were encouraged to adopt the role of "Preschooler's Door to Learning" as a priority; center children's services around the developmental needs of children and their families; and build coalitions and develop a shared vision with the early-care and education community. The prototype emphasized the library's role in reaching families and stated that library programs should be family-based. For those families not already coming to the library, outreach is necessary. It is time, as Alice Scott, Assistant Commissioner for Systemwide Services of the Chicago Public Library, states in an article for *Illinois Libraries,* that outreach no longer be seen as a stepchild of, but as part of a library's ongoing program of service.[15] Then, and only then, will the library serve all the families in a community.

ENDNOTES

1. Phyllis Chandler, *A Place for Me: Including Children With Special Needs in Early Care and Education Settings.* (Washington, D.C.: National Association for the Education of Young Children, 1994), p. 5.

2. Ibid., pp. 7-8.

3. Library Service to Children With Special Needs Committee, Association for Library Service to Children, *Programming for Serving Children With Special Needs.* (Chicago: American Library Association, 1994).

4. Ann D. Carlson, *The Preschooler and the Library.* (Metuchen, N.J.: Scarecrow, 1991).

5. Kieth C. Wright, *Serving the Disabled: A How-To-Do It Manual.* (New York: Neal-Schuman, 1991).

6. National Center for Education Statistics, *Language Characteristics and Schooling in the United States: A Changing Picture: 1979 and 1989.* (Washington, D.C.: U.S Department of Education, 1994). Stock no. 065-000-00623-5.

7. Aaron Epstein, "Those are Fighting Words, Amigo," *Youngstown (Ohio) Vindicator,* June 12, 1994, City Edition (from a Census Bureau report).

8. George E. Morrison, *Early Childhood Education Today.* 5th ed. (New York: Macmillan, 1991), p. 285.

9. Children's Defense Fund, *The State of America's Children Yearbook 1994.* (Washington, D.C.: Children's Defense Fund, 1994), p. 38.

10. Mary A. Landgraf, "Library Cards for the Homeless," *American Libraries,* November 1991: 946-949.

11. Children's Defense Fund, *The State of America's Children Yearbook 1994.* (Washington, D.C.: Children's Defense Fund, 1994), p. 2.

12. Sue McCleaf Nespeca, *Parental Involvement in Emergent Literacy Skills of Urban Head Start Children.* (Kent State University, unpublished, 1991).

13. Marcella Anderson, *Books and Children in Pediatric Settings: A Guide for Caregivers and Librarians.* (Metuchen, N.J.: Scarecrow Press, 1992).

14. Children's Defense Fund, *The State of America's Children Yearbook 1994.* (Washington, D.C.: Children's Defense Fund, 1994), p. 54.

15. Alice H. Scott, "Outreach: No Longer the Stepchild," *Illinois Libraries* 75 (Fall 1993): 304-306.

INDEX

Sue McCleaf Nespeca is Youth Services Coordinator for NOLA Regional Library System, a consortium of over 80 public, school, academic and special libraries in eight counties of northeast Ohio. In addition to a M.L.S., she has her Masters in Early Childhood Education. Active in ALA's Association For Library Service to Children Division, and is presently chair of the Library/Head Start Partnership Task Force and convener for the Preschool Services Discussion Group. Nespeca was also a member of the 1993 Caldecott Committee and contributed to the ALA publication First Steps to Literacy: Library Programs for Parents, Teachers and Caregivers. As the first recipient of the Bechtel Fellowship sponsored by ALSC and the University of Florida, she studied historical children's literature at the Baldwin Library.